W9-BHN-070

FROM

FORT HENRY TO CORINTH

FROM

FORT HENRY TO CORINTH

BY

M. F. FORCE

LATE BRIGADIER–GENERAL AND BREVET MAJOR-GENERAL, U. S. V.,
COMMANDING FIRST DIVISION, SEVENTEENTH CORPS.

CASTLE BOOKS

CAMPAIGNS OF THE CIVIL WAR.—II.
FROM FORT HENRY TO CORINTH

This edition published in 2002 by Castle Books,
A division of Book Sales Inc.
114 Northfield Avenue, Edison, NJ 08837

First published in 1881.
Written by M.F. Force.

ISBN: 0-7858-1574-0

Printed in the United States of America.

PREFACE.

I HAVE endeavored to prepare the following narrative from authentic material, contemporaneous, or nearly contemporaneous, with the events described.

The main source of information is the official reports of battles and operations. These reports, both National and Confederate, will appear in the series of volumes of Military Reports now in preparation under the supervision of Colonel Scott, Chief of the War Records Office in the War Department. Executive Document No. 66, printed by resolution of the Senate at the Second Session of the Thirty-seventh Congress, contains a number of separate reports of casualties, lists of killed, wounded, and missing, which do not appear in the volumes of Military Reports as now printed. Several battle reports are printed in volume IV., and in the "Companion," or Appendix volume of Moore's Rebellion Record, which are not contained in the volumes of Military Reports as now printed. The reports of the Twentieth Ohio and the Fifty-third Ohio, of the battle of Shiloh, have never been printed. Colonel Trabue's report of his brigade in the battle of Shiloh has never been officially printed; but it is

given in the history of the Kentucky Brigade from Colonel
Trabue's retained copy, found by his widow among his
papers.

The Reports of the Committee on the Conduct of the War
contain original matter in addition to what appears in reports of battles and operations.

The reports of the Adjutant-Generals of the different
States, printed during the war, often supplement the official
reports on file in Washington.

Some regimental histories, printed soon after the close of
the war, contain diaries and letters and narrate incidents
which enable us in some cases to fix dates, the place of
camps, and positions in battle, which could hardly otherwise
be determined with precision. Newspaper correspondents,
while narrating what they personally saw, give descriptions
which impart animation to the sedate statements of official
reports.

Colonel William Preston Johnston's life of his father,
General A. S. Johnston, can be used in some respects as authority. He served first in the Army of Northern Virginia, and was, most of the war, on the staff of Jefferson
Davis. He thus, after his father's death, became possessed
of a valuable collection of authentic official papers. When
he was preparing the biography, all papers of value in
private hands in the South were open to his use.

Letters and memoranda preserved by Colonel Charles
Whittlesey, and some of my own, have been of service.

I am under obligation to Colonel Scott for permission to
freely read and copy, in his office, the reports compiled under
his direction. To Ex-President Hayes for the loan of a set

of the series of Military Reports, both National and Confederate, so far as printed, though not yet issued. To the Historical and Philosophical Society of Ohio for the unrestricted use of its library. To Colonel Charles Whittlesey of Cleveland, and Major E. C. Dawes, of Cincinnati, for the use of original manuscripts as well as printed reports.

M. F. FORCE.

CONTENTS.

LIST OF MAPS.

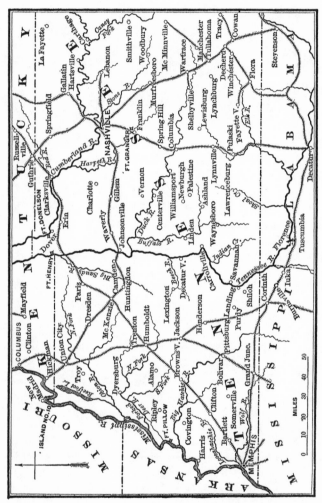

Western Tennessee.

FROM FORT HENRY TO CORINTH.

CHAPTER I.

PRELIMINARY.

MISSOURI did not join the Southern States in their secession from the Union. A convention called to consider the question passed resolutions opposed to the movement. But the legislature convened by Governor Jackson gave him dictatorial power, authorized him especially to organize the military power of the State, and put into his hands three millions of dollars, diverted from the funds to which they had been appropriated, to complete the armament. The governor divided the State into nine military districts, appointed a brigadier-general to each, and appointed Sterling Price major-general.

The convention reassembled in July, 1861, and, by action subject to disapproval or affirmance of the popular vote, deposed the governor, lieutenant-governor, secretary of state, and legislature, and appointed a new executive. This action was approved by a vote of the people. Jackson, assuming to be an ambulatory government as he chased about with forces alternately advancing and fleeing, undertook, by his separate act, to detach Missouri from the Union and annex it to the Confederacy.

II.—1

This clash of action stimulated and intensified a real division of feeling, which existed in every county. A sputtering warfare broke out all over the State. Armed predatory parties, rebel and national, calling themselves squadrons, battalions, regiments, springing up as if from the ground, whirled into conflict and vanished. When a band of men without uniform, wearing their ordinary dress and carrying their own arms, dispersed over the country, the separate members could not be distinguished from other farmers or villagers; and a train, being merely a collection of country wagons, if scattered among the stables and barn-yards of the adjoining territory, wholly disappeared. But all through this eruptive discord flowed a continuous stream of more regular contests, which constitute the connected beginning of the military operations of the Mississippi Valley.

Under countenance of Governor Jackson's proclamation, General D. M. Frost organized a force and established Camp Jackson, near St. Louis, the site being now covered by a well-built portion of the city. Jackson had refused to call out troops in response to President Lincoln's requisition, but Frank P. Blair had promptly raised one regiment and stimulated the formation of four others in St. Louis. On May 10, 1861, Captain Nathaniel Lyon, of the regular army, who commanded at the arsenal at St. Louis, and had there a garrison of several hundred regulars, marched with Colonel Blair and the volunteers and a battery to Camp Jackson, surrounded it, and demanded a surrender. Resistance was useless. General Frost surrendered his men and stores, including twenty cannon. St. Louis, and with it Missouri, was thus preserved. Lyon was made brigadier-general of volunteers.

Jackson and Price left Jefferson City—Jackson stopping, on June 18th, at Booneville, one rendezvous for his forces,

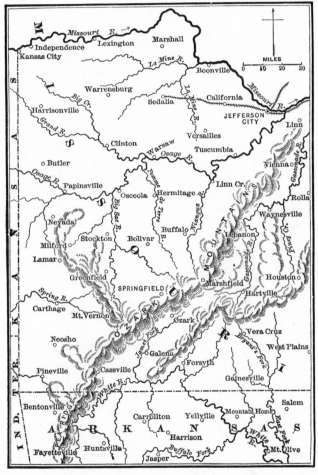

The Field of Operations in Missouri and Northern Arkansas.

while Price continued up the river to Lexington, another rendezvous. General Lyon, leaving St. Louis on June 13th with an expeditionary force on boats, reached Booneville almost as soon as Jackson. The unorganized and partially armed gathering of several thousand men made an impotent attempt at resistance when Lyon landed, but was quickly routed. Jackson fled, with his mounted men and such of the infantry as he could hold together, to the southwest part of the State, gathering accretions of men as he marched. Lyon set out in pursuit, and Price, abandoning Lexington, hastened with the force assembled there to join Jackson. Colonel Franz Sigel had proceeded from St. Louis to Rolla by rail, and marched thence in pursuit of Jackson to strike him before he could be reinforced. Sigel, with 1,500 men, encountered Jackson with more than double that number, on July 5th, near Carthage, in Jasper County. Sigel's superiority in artillery gave him an advantage in a desultory combat of some hours. Jackson, greatly outnumbering him in cavalry, proceeded to envelop his rear, and Sigel was forced to withdraw. Sigel retreated in perfect order, and managed his artillery so well that the pursuing cavalry were kept at a distance, while he marched with his train through Carthage, and fifteen miles beyond, before halting. That night and next morning Jackson was heavily reinforced by Price, who brought from the south several thousand Arkansas and Texas troops, under General Ben. McCulloch and General Pearce. Sigel continued his retreat to Springfield, where he was joined by General Lyon on July 10th.

Price and McCulloch being continually reinforced, largely with cavalry, overran Southwestern Missouri. Lyon waited in vain for reinforcements, and, having but little cavalry, kept closely to the vicinity of Springfield. Learning that the enemy were marching upon him in two strong columns, one from the south and one from the west, he moved out from Springfield with all his force on August 1st, and early next morning encountered at Dug Springs a portion of the column advancing from the south under McCulloch. This detachment was shattered and dispersed, and McCulloch recoiled and moved to the west, to join Price commanding the other column. Price advanced slowly with the combined force and went into camp on Wilson Creek, ten miles south of Springfield, on August 7th.

Lyon's entire force was, upon the rolls, 5,868. This number included sick, wounded, and detached on special duty. General Price turned over his Missouri troops and relinquished command to McCulloch. According to Price's official report, his Missourians engaged in the battle of the 10th were 5,221. According to the official report of McCulloch, his entire effective force was 5,300 infantry, 15 pieces of artillery, 6,000 horsemen armed with flintlock muskets, rifles, and shotguns, and a number of unarmed horsemen.

General Lyon, not having sufficient force to retreat across the open country to supports, resolved to strike a sharp blow that would cripple his opponent, and thus secure an unmolested retreat. He marched out from Springfield at five o'clock P.M., on August 9th, leaving 250 men and one gun as a guard. Colonel Sigel, with 1,200 men and a battery of six pieces, moved to the left, to get into the rear of McCulloch's right flank; Lyon, with 3,700 men, including two batteries, Totten's with six guns, and Dubois with four, and also including two battalions of regular infantry, inclined to the right so as to come upon the centre of the enemy's front. The columns came in sight of McCulloch's camp-fires after midnight, and rested in place till day. At six o'clock on the morning of the 10th, attack was made almost simultaneously by the two columns at the points designated. Sigel advanced to the attack with great gallantry, but soon suffered a disastrous repulse ; five of his six guns were taken and his command scattered.

McCulloch's entire force, with artillery increased by the five pieces taken from Sigel, turned upon Lyon's little command. Lyon's men were well posted and fought with extraordinary steadiness. Infantry and artillery face to face fired at each other, with occasional intermissions, nearly six hours. General Lyon, after being twice wounded, was killed. The opposing lines at times came almost in contact. Each side at times recoiled. When the conflict reached the hottest, and McCulloch pushed his men, about eleven o'clock, up almost to the muzzles of the national line, Captain Granger rushed to the rear, brought up the supports of Dubois' battery, eight companies in all, being portions of the First Kansas, First Missouri, and the First Iowa, fell suddenly upon McCulloch's right flank, and opened a fire that shot away a portion of McCulloch's line. This cross-fire cleared that portion of the field ; McCulloch's whole line gave way and retired out of view. It was now for the first time safe for Major Sturgis, who had assumed command on the death of Lyon, to retreat. Sturgis withdrew in order and fell back to Springfield unmolested. The entire national loss, according to the official report, was 223 killed, 721 wounded, and 292 missing. The missing were nearly all from Sigel's column. Two regiments in General Lyon's column, the First Missouri and the First Kansas, lost together 153 killed and 395 wounded. General Price reported the loss of his Missouri troops, 156 killed, 517 wounded, and 30 missing. General McCulloch reported his entire loss as 265 killed, 800 wounded, and 30 missing. The death of General Lyon was a severe loss. He was zealous in the national cause and enterprising in maintaining it ; he was ready to assume responsibility, and prompt in taking initiative ; sagacious in comprehending his antagonist, quick in decision, fertile in resource, and was as cool as he was bold. On the night of the 10th, the army stores in Springfield were put into the wagons, and next morning the national force set out for Rolla, the end of the railroad, where it arrived in good order on the 15th. Meanwhile, Price and McCulloch, having some disagreement, withdrew to the Arkansas border.

General John C. Fremont was, July 9, 1861, assigned to the command of the Western District, comprising the States of Illinois, Kentucky, Missouri, and Kansas, and territories west, and arrived in St. Louis from the East on July 25th. Before arriving he appointed Brigadier-General John Pope to command the district of Northern Missouri, being that part of Missouri north of the Missouri River. Pope arrived at St. Charles, Mo., with three infantry regiments and part of one cavalry regiment of Illinois volunteers, on July 17th, and assumed command. On July 21st, General Pope published an order making all property within five miles of a railway responsible for malicious injury done to such railway. On July 31st he published another order, making the property of each county responsible for damage done by, and the cost of suppressing, predatory outbreaks in such county. For a month the effect of these orders was to allay disturbance in the district, and secure the administration of affairs by the ordinary machinery of civil government ; but in about a month the orders were set aside, and in their place martial law was declared throughout the State.

General Fremont learned of the battle of Wilson Creek on August 13th, and resolved at once to fortify St. Louis as his permanent base, and also fortify and garrison Jefferson City, Rolla, Cape Girardeau, and Ironton. Price marched leisurely up through the western border of the State. Unorganized

bands springing up in the country attacked Booneville and
Lexington, but were easily repulsed by the little detachments guarding those places.   Colonel Mulligan was sent to
Lexington with additional troops, making the entire force
there 2,800 men and eight field-pieces, and with orders to
remain until relieved or reinforced.

On September 11th, Price arrived before Lexington.
There is no authentic report of his strength ; indeed, a large
part of his following was an unorganized assemblage.   He
must have numbered 14,000 men at the beginning of the
siege ; and reinforcements daily arriving swelled the number
to, at all events, more than 20,000.   Colonel Mulligan took
position on a rising ground close to the river, east of the city,
forming a plateau with a surface of about fifteen acres, and
fortified.

Judging by the despatches of General Fremont, he seems
to have felt no apprehension as to the fate of Mulligan, and
made no serious effort to relieve him.   The force at Jefferson
City remained there.   The troops at St. Louis were not moved.
General Pope, who, under orders from General Fremont,
had advanced from Hannibal to St. Joseph along the line of
the railroad, driving off depredators, repairing the road, and
stationing permanent guards, heard on September 16th, at
Palmyra on his return, something of the condition of affairs
at Lexington.   He had sent his troops then in the western
part of the State toward the Missouri River in pursuit of a
depredating body of the enemy.   He immediately despatched
an order to these troops to hasten to Lexington upon completing their present business.   They were not able, however, to arrive in time.

Price, having organized his command into five divisions,
each commanded by a general officer, did not push his siege
vigorously till the 18th.   On that day, a force proceeding

through the city of Lexington and under cover of the river-bank, seized the ferry-boats, cut Mulligan off from his water-supply, and carried a mansion close to Mulligan's works and overlooking them. A sortie and a desperate struggle regained possession of the house. Another assault and another desperate struggle finally dispossessed the garrison of the house. Price closed in upon the beleaguered works and firing became continuous and uninterrupted. On the 20th, Price, having a footing on the plateau, carried up numbers of bales of hemp and used them as a movable entrenchment. By rolling these forward, he pushed his line close to Mulligan's works. The besieged were already suffering from want of water, and surrender could be no longer postponed.

Fremont, hearing of the surrender on September 22d, began to bestir himself to look after Price. He left St. Louis for Jefferson City on the 27th, and sent thither the regiments that had been kept at St. Louis. Price on the same day moved out of Lexington and marched deliberately to the southwest corner of the State. On September 24th, Fremont published an order constructing an army for the field of five divisions, entitled right wing, centre, left wing, advance, and reserve—under the command, respectively, of Generals Pope, McKinstry, Hunter, Sigel, and Ashboth; headquarters being respectively at Booneville, Syracuse, Versailles, Georgetown, and Tipton. The regiments and batteries assigned to the respective divisions were scattered all over the State, many of them without wagons, mules, over-coats, cartridge-boxes, or rations. Orders were issued to advance and concentrate at Springfield. Sigel arrived there on the evening of October 27th, and Ashboth on the 30th. Fremont was convinced that Price was on Wilson's Creek, ten or twelve miles from Springfield. Despatches were sent urging McKinstry, Hunter, and Pope to hasten. Pope, having marched seventy miles in two days, arrived on November 1st, and McKinstry arrived close behind him.

On November 2d an order came from Washington relieving Fremont from command of the department, and appointing Hunter to the command. Hunter having not yet come up, Fremont held a council of war, exhibited his plan of battle at Wilson Creek, and ordered advance and attack to be made next morning. General Hunter arrived in the night and assumed command. He sent a reconnoissance next day to Wilson Creek, and learned that no enemy was there or had been there. It was soon ascertained that Price was at Cassville, more than sixty miles off. The army being without rations and imperfectly supplied with transportation, General Hunter, acting upon his own judgment and also in accordance with the wish of President Lincoln expressed in a letter to him, refrained from any attempt to overtake Price, and withdrew his army back to the railroads.

On November 9th, General Halleck was appointed commander of the new Department of the Missouri, including that portion of Kentucky west of the Cumberland River. One-half of the force which Fremont had assembled at Springfield was stationed along the railway from Jefferson City to Sedalia, its western terminus, and General Pope was put in command of this force, as well as a district designated Central Missouri. General Price advanced into Missouri as far as Osceola, on the southern bank of the Osage River, from which point he sent parties in various directions, and where he received detachments of recruits. On December 15th, Pope moved out from Sedalia directly to the south, as if he were pushing for Warsaw, and at the same time sent a cavalry force to the southwest, to mask his movement from Price's command at and near Osceola. Next day a forced march took him west to a position south of Warrensburg, and between the two roads leading from Warrensburg to Osceola. The same night he captured the pickets, and thereby learned the precise locality of a body of 3,200 men, moving from Lexington south to join Price. A flying column under Lieutenant-Colonel Brown, sent out the same night, came upon the camp, drove out the command, kept up the pursuit all night, and all the next day and night, pushing the fugitives away from Price and utterly dispersing them over the country, and rejoined Pope on the 18th with 150 prisoners, and sixteen wagons loaded with supplies captured. At the same time Major Hubbard with his detachment pushed south to the lines of one of Price's divisions, encamped opposite Osceola, on the north shore of the Osage, and captured pickets and one entire company of cavalry, with its tents and wagons. On the 18th, Pope moved to the north, to intercept another body moving south to join Price, and which he learned from his scouts would camp that night at the mouth of Clear Creek, just beyond Warrensburg. His dispositions were so made and carried out that the entire body was surrounded and captured, comprising parts of two regiments of infantry and three companies of cavalry—numbering 1,300 officers and men, with complete train and full supplies. Pope's troops reoccupied their camps at Sedalia and Otterville just one week after they marched out of them. Price broke up his camp at Osceola in haste, and fell rapidly back to Springfield.

General Samuel R. Curtis arrived at Rolla on December 27th, to take command of a force concentrating there and called the Army of the Southwest. One division, under the command of Colonel Jefferson C. Davis, detached from General Pope's district, added to three other divisions commanded respectively by General Sigel, General Ashboth, and

Colonel E. A. Carr, made together 12,095 men and fifty pieces of artillery, including four mountain howitzers. Marching out from Rolla on January 23, 1862, with three divisions, he halted a week at Lebanon, where he was joined by Colonel Davis, completing organization and preparation. After some skirmishing with Price's outposts, Curtis entered Springfield at daylight, February 15th, to find that Price had abandoned it in the night. Curtis followed with forced marches, his advance skirmishing every day with Price's rear-guard. In Arkansas, Price was joined by McCulloch and they retired to Boston Mountains. Curtis advanced as far as Fayetteville and then fell back to await attack on ground of his own choice.

The position selected was where the main road, running north from Fayetteville into Missouri, crosses Sugar Creek, and goes over a ridge or rough plateau called Pea Ridge, and was near the Missouri line. For easier subsistence the divisions were camped separately and some miles apart. Davis' division was at Sugar Creek, preparing the position for defence. Sigel, with his own and Ashboth's divisions, was at Cooper's farm, about fourteen miles west; and Carr's division, with which General Curtis had his headquarters, was twelve miles south on the main Fayetteville road, at a place called Cross Hollows. Strong detachments were sent in various directions, forty miles out, to gather in forage and subsistence. The strength of the command was somewhat diminished by the necessity of protecting the long line of communication with the base of supplies by patrols as well as stationary guards, and the aggregate present in Arkansas was 10,500 infantry and cavalry, and forty-nine pieces of artillery.

To settle the continued dissension between Price and Mc-Culloch, General A. S. Johnston, the Confederate commander in the West, appointed General Earl Van Dorn to command west of the Mississippi. Van Dorn assumed command January 29, 1862, in northeastern Arkansas, and hastened on February 22d to join McCulloch at Fayetteville, to which place Price was then retreating before Curtis. Van Dorn says that he led 14,000 men into action. All other accounts put his force at from thirty to forty thousand. Perhaps he enumerated only the seasoned regiments, and took no account of unorganized bands, or of the several thousand Indians under Albert Pike.

At two o'clock P.M., March 5th, General Curtis received intelligence that Van Dorn had begun his march. Orders were immediately sent to the divisions and detachments to concentrate on Davis' division. Carr moved at 6 P.M., and arrived at 2 A.M. Sigel deferred moving till two o'clock A.M., and at Bentonville halted, himself with a regiment of infantry, the Twelfth Missouri, Elbert's light battery, and five companies of cavalry, till ten o'clock, two hours after the rear of his train had passed through the place. By this time Van Dorn's advance guard had arrived, and before Sigel could form had passed around to his front, at the same time enveloping his flanks. By the skilful disposition of his detachment, and the admirable conduct of the men, Sigel was able to resume and continue his march, an unbroken skirmish, rising at times into engagement, from half-past ten o'clock till half-past three, when he was joined by reinforcements which General Curtis had hurried back to him. The line was formed, facing to the south, on the crest of the bluffs overlooking the Valley of Sugar Creek, Sigel being on the right, next to him Ashboth, then Davis, and Carr being the left. The position was entrenched, and the approaches were obstructed by felled timber. One foraging party of 250 men and one gun did not return till after the battle, so that Curtis' force engaged was just 10,250 men and forty-eight guns.

Van Dorn did not assault that evening. By dawn next day it was ascertained that he had made a great detour by the west, and was coming up on the right and rear. Curtis faced his line to the rear and wheeled to the left, so that his new line faced nearly west; the original right flank, now the left, was scarcely moved, and Carr's division had become the right. Colonel Osterhaus, with three regiments of infantry and two batteries, was despatched from Sigel's division to aid a regiment of cavalry and a flying battery that had been quickly sent to retard the enemy's centre and give Carr's division time to deploy. Osterhaus met the cavalry returning, and threw his detachment against the advancing line. The picket posted at Elkhorn tavern, where Carr was to deploy, was attacked and driven back, and Carr's division had to go into line under fire. Osterhaus found himself opposed to the corps of McCulloch and McIntosh, and was about being overwhelmed when Davis' division moved to his support. Pea Ridge is in places covered with timber and brush, in places intersected by deep ravines, and a portion of it was a tangle of fallen timber, marking the path of a hurricane. Manœuvring was not easy, and detours were required in reinforcing one part of the line from another. The contest on the field, where Davis and Osterhaus were opposed to McCulloch and McIntosh, was fierce and determined until McCulloch and McIntosh were killed. Their numerous, but partially disciplined followers lost heart and direction, and before the close of day gave way before the persistent and orderly attack, and finally broke and left the field.

Carr's division was opposed to Price's corps, and Van Dorn gave his personal attention to that part of the field. Gallantry and determination could not prevail against gallantry and determination backed by superior numbers. Bit by bit, first on one flank, then the other, he receded. Curtis sent his body-guard, then the camp-guard to reinforce him, and then a small reserve that had been guarding the road to the rear. Carr had sent word he could not hold out much longer. Curtis sent word to persevere, and went in person to the left, where Sigel with his two divisions had not yet been under fire, and hurried Ashboth over to Carr's relief. Carr had been gradually pushed back nearly a mile; Van Dorn had been concentrating upon him, resolved to crush him. Curtis, returning with Ashboth, met the Fourth Iowa marching to the rear, in good order. Colonel Dodge explained that ammunition was exhausted, and he was going for cartridges. "Then use your bayonets," was the reply, and the regiment faced again to the enemy and steadily advanced. It was about five o'clock P.M. when Ashboth reached Carr's line and immediately opened fire. The combat continued till dark set in.

As it was evident that Van Dorn was throwing his whole force upon the position held by Carr, General Curtis took advantage of the cessation during the night to re-form his line. Davis and Osterhaus were brought to join Carr's left, and Sigel was ordered to form on the left of Osterhaus. When the sun rose, Sigel was not yet in position, but Davis and Carr began attack without waiting. General Curtis, riding to the front of Carr's right, found in advance a rising ground which gave a commanding position for a battery, posted the Dubuque battery there, and moved forward the right to its support. Sigel, coming up with the divisions of Osterhaus and Ashboth on Davis' left, first sent a battery forward, which by its rapid fire repelled the enemy in its front, and then with its deployed supports wheeled half to the right. Another battery pushed forward repeated the manœuvre with its supporting infantry. The column thus deployed on the right into line, bending back the enemy's right wing in the execution of the movement—each step in the deployment gaining space for the next succeeding step. The line as now formed, from the Dubuque battery on the right to Sigel's left, formed a curve enclosing Van Dorn's army. Under this concentric fire Van Dorn's entire force before noon was swept from the field to find refuge in the deep and tortuous ravines in his rear. Pursuit was fruitless. McCulloch's command, scattering in all directions, was irretrievably dispersed. Van Dorn, with Price's corps and other troops, found outlet by a ravine leading to the south, unobserved by the national troops, went into camp ten miles off on the prairie, and sent in a flag of truce to bury his dead. The national loss was 203 killed, 972 wounded, and 176 missing. Van Dorn reported his loss as 600 killed and wounded and 200 prisoners, but the dispersion of a large portion of his command prevented full reports.

Van Dorn was now ordered to report at Corinth, where A. S. Johnston was assembling his army. Most of the national forces remaining in Missouri were sent to General Grant, to aid in his expeditions against Fort Henry and Fort Donelson. General Curtis made a promenade across Arkansas, halting at times, and came out on the Mississippi in July, 1862.

While Price kept Southwest Missouri in a state of alarm, Jefferson Thompson, appointed by Governor Jackson brigadier-general and commander of district, marauded over Southeastern Missouri, sometimes raiding far enough to the north to strike and damage railways. On October 14, 1861, by a rapid march he passed by Pilot Knob, which Colonel Carlin held with 1,500 men, struck the Iron Mountain Railroad at its crossing of Big River, destroyed the bridge—the largest bridge on the road—and immediately fell back to Fredericktown. The news reaching St. Louis on the 15th, the Eighth Wisconsin infantry and Schofield's battery were despatched thence to reinforce Colonel Carlin; and General Grant, commanding at Cape Girardeau, sent Colonel Plummer, of the Eleventh Missouri, with his own regiment, the Seventeenth and Twentieth Illinois, a section of artillery and two companies of cavalry, in all 1,500 men, to join in an attack upon Thompson. Meanwhile a party of cavalry was sent out from Pilot Knob to Fredericktown, to occupy Thompson by demonstrations and hold him there.

Colonel Plummer marched out from Cape Girardeau on the morning of the 18th, and sent a messenger to Colonel Carlin advising him of his movement; the messenger fell into Thompson's hands. Thompson sent his train to the south, and, moving a few miles below Fredericktown with his force numbering 4,000 men, took a strong position and awaited attack. Carlin with 3,000 men effected a junction with Plummer and his 1,500, the combined force being under command of Colonel Plummer. Thompson was attacked as soon as discovered. After a sharp fight of two hours Thompson gave way, was driven from his position, retreated, and fell into rout. He was pursued several miles that day, and the pursuing force returned to Fredericktown for the night. Next day Colonel Plummer followed in pursuit twenty-two miles without further result, returned to Fredericktown the 23d, and on the 24th began his march back to Cape Girardeau.

Colonel Plummer's loss was 6 killed and 60 wounded. He took 80 prisoners, 38 of them wounded; captured one iron twelve-pounder gun, a number of small arms and horses, and buried 158 of Thompson's dead before leaving Fredericktown. Thompson's following was demoralized by this defeat, and Southeast Missouri after it enjoyed comparative quiet.

2

The State of Kentucky at first undertook to hold the position of armed neutrality in the civil war. On September 4, 1861, Gen. Leonidas Polk, moving up from Tennessee with a considerable force into Western Kentucky, seized Hickman and Columbus on the Mississippi, and threatened Paducah on the Ohio. Gen. Ulysses S. Grant, appointed brigadier-general of volunteers on August 7, 1861, to date from May 17th, assumed command on September 1st, by order of General Fremont, of the District of Southeast Missouri. This district included not only the southeastern part of Missouri, but also Southern Illinois, and so much of Western Kentucky and Tennessee as might fall into possession of the national forces. General Grant arrived at Cairo on September 2d, established his headquarters there on the 4th, and next day heard of the action of General Polk. He immediately notified General Fremont, and also the Legislature of Kentucky, then in session at Frankfort, of the fact. Getting further information in the day, he telegraphed to General Fremont he would go to Paducah unless orders to the contrary should be received. He started in the night with two regiments and a battery, and arrived at Paducah at half-past six next morning. General L. Tilghman being in the city with his staff and a single company of recruits, hurried away by rail, and Grant occupied the city without opposition. The Legislature passed a resolution "that Kentucky expects the Confederate or Tennessee troops to be withdrawn from her soil unconditionally." Polk remained, and Kentucky as a State was ranged in support of the government.

General Grant, leaving a sufficient garrison, returned at noon to Cairo to find there permission from Fremont to take Paducah if he felt strong enough, and also a reprimand for communicating directly with a legislature. General C. F. Smith was put in command of Paducah next day by Fremont, with orders to report directly to Fremont. A few weeks later, Smith occupied and garrisoned Smithland at the mouth of the Cumberland. Grant suggested the feasibility of capturing Columbus, and on September 10th asked permission to make the attempt. No notice was taken of the request. His command was, however, continually reinforced by new regiments, and he found occupation in organizing and disciplining them. General Polk meanwhile was busy fortifying Columbus, where the river-bank rises to a high bluff, until the bluff was faced and crowned with massive earthworks, armed with one hundred and forty-two pieces of artillery, mostly thirty-two and sixty-four pounders. At the same time heavy defensive works commanding the river were erected below at Island No. Ten and New Madrid, and still farther below, but above Memphis, at Fort Pillow.

On November 1st, General Fremont being on his expedition to Springfield, his adjutant in charge of headquarters at St. Louis directed General Grant to make demonstrations on both sides of the Mississippi at Norfolk, Charleston, and Blandville, points a few miles north of Columbus and Belmont. Next day he advised Grant that Jeff. Thompson was at Indian Ford of the St. François River, twenty-five miles below Greenville, with about three thousand men, and that Colonel Carlin had started from Pilot Knob in pursuit, and directing Grant to send a force to assist Carlin in driving Thompson into Arkansas. On the night of the 3d, Grant despatched Colonel Oglesby with 3,000 men from Commerce to carry out this order. On the 5th, Grant was further advised by telegraph that General Polk, who commanded at Columbus, was sending reinforcements to Price, and that it was of vital importance that this movement should be arrested. General Grant at once sent an additional regiment to Oglesby, with directions to him to turn his course to the

river in the direction of New Madrid; requested General C.
F. Smith to make a demonstration from Paducah toward
Columbus; and also sent parties from Bird's Point and Fort
Holt to move down both sides of the river, so as to attract
attention from Columbus.

On the evening of the 6th, General Grant started down the
river on transports with five regiments of infantry, the Twenty-second, Twenty-seventh, Thirtieth, and Thirty-first Illinois, and the Seventh Iowa, Taylor's Chicago battery, and
two companies of cavalry. The Twenty-seventh, Thirtieth,
and Thirty-first Illinois were made into a brigade commanded by General John A. McClernand; the Twenty-second
Illinois and the Seventh Iowa into a brigade under Colonel H.
Dougherty, of the Twenty-second Illinois. The entire force
numbered 3,114 men. General Grant, in his report, states the
number at 2,850. As five companies were kept at the landing when the force disembarked, the number given by General Grant represents the number taken into action. Two
gunboats, under the command of Captain Walke of the navy,
convoyed the expedition. A feint was made of landing
nine miles below Cairo, on the Kentucky side, and the expedition lay there till daybreak. Badeau says that General
Grant received intelligence, at two o'clock in the morning
of the 7th, that General Polk was crossing troops from Columbus to Belmont, with a view of cutting off Oglesby, and
that he thereupon determined to convert what had been
intended as a mere demonstration against Belmont into a
real attack.

Belmont was the lofty name of a settlement of three
houses squatted upon the low river-flat opposite Columbus,
and under easy range of its guns. A regiment and a battery
were encamped in a cleared field of seven hundred acres on
the river-bank, and the camp was surrounded on its land-

ward side by an abattis of felled timber. At six o'clock in the morning the fleet moved down, and the troops debarked at half-past eight on the Missouri shore, three miles above Columbus, and protected from view by an intervening wooded point. About the same time General Polk sent General Pillow across the river to Belmont with four regiments, making the force there five regiments and a battery. Pillow estimated the number of men at about twenty-five hundred.

General Grant marched his command through the timber and some cleared fields, and formed in two lines facing the river—McClernand in front, Dougherty in rear. A depression parallel to the river, making a connected series of ponds or sloughs, had to be crossed in the advance in line. These depressions were for the most part dry, but the Twenty-seventh Illinois, the right of the front line, in passing around a portion that was yet filled with water, made such distance to the right that Colonel Dougherty's brigade moved forward, filled the interval, and the attack was made in a single line.

The opposing skirmishers encountered in the timber. Pillow's line of battle was in the open, facing the timber. The engagement was in the simplest form : two forces equal in number encountered in parallel lines. Most of the men on both sides were for the first time under fire, and had yet had but scanty opportunity to become inured to or acquainted with military discipline. The engagement was hotly contested—the opposing lines, while for some time alternately advancing and receding, were steady and unbroken. At length Pillow gave way. When his line was once really broken it could not rally in the face of pursuit. The national line pressing on, pushed Pillow back through the camp and over the upper or secondary bank to the first or lower bottom in disorder. The Second Tennessee, just arrived across the river, took position under the secondary bank, for a while checked the pursuit, giving time for the routed troops to make their way through the timber up the river, and finally followed them in a more orderly retreat.

The national troops, having now undisturbed possession of the captured camp, gave way to their exultation. General McClernand called for three cheers, that were given with a will. The regiments broke ranks, and the battery fired upon the massive works and heavy siege-guns crowning the heights across the river. A plunging fire of great shells from the fortifications, and the sight of boats loaded with troops leaving the opposite shore, were impressive warnings that the invaders could not safely tarry. General Grant directed the camp to be set on fire, and the command to be assembled and to return. General Polk became convinced that Columbus was not in danger of present attack, and determined to reinforce Pillow promptly and effectively. The Eleventh Louisiana and Fifteenth Tennessee arrived first, and attack was made upon both flanks of the hastily formed retreating column, encumbered as it was with spoils. The Seventh Iowa and Twenty-second Illinois, the regiments mainly attacked, replied with vigor, though thrown into some confusion. Pillow halted his men to re-form, and drew them off to await the arrival of reinforcements on the way, under General Polk in person.

The command embarked. The battery took on board two guns and a wagon captured and brought off in place of two caissons and a wagon left behind, and also brought off twenty horses and one mule captured. When all who were in sight were on board, General Grant, supposing the five companies who had been left to guard the landing were still on post, rode out to look for one of the parties that had been sent to bring in the wounded, and which had not returned. Instead of the guard, which had gone on board without or-

ders, supposing its duty was done, he saw approaching a
hostile line of battle. He rode back, his horse slid down
the river-bank on its haunches, and trotted on board a transport over a plank thrust out for him. General Polk had
come over with General Cheatham, bringing two more regiments and a battalion. The entire force formed in line,
approached the river-bank, and opened fire. The gunboats,
as well as the infantry on the transports, returned the fire.
Each side was confident that its fire caused great slaughter;
but, in fact, little damage was done. The fleet, some distance up-stream, overtook and received on board the Twenty-seventh Illinois, which had become separated from the
column, and, instead of returning with it, returned by the
road over which the advance was made. The national loss
was: in McClernand's brigade, 30 killed, 130 wounded, and
54 missing; in Dougherty's brigade, 49 killed, 154 wounded,
and 63 missing; in Taylor's battery, 5 wounded. There
were no casualties in the cavalry. The aggregate loss was
79 killed, 289 wounded, and 117 missing; making, in all,
485. Most of the wounded were left behind and taken prisoners. A number of the missing made their way to Cairo.
The Seventh Iowa suffered most severely. Among the 26
killed and 80 wounded were the lieutenant-colonel killed,
and the colonel and major wounded. Colonel Dougherty,
of the Twenty-second Illinois, commanding the second brigade, was wounded and taken prisoner. The Confederate
loss was 105 killed, 419 wounded, and 117 missing; in all,
641. Of this aggregate, 562 were from the five regiments
originally engaged. Besides the loss in men and the destruction of the camp, forty-five horses were killed.

CHAPTER II.

FORT HENRY.

GENERAL A. S. JOHNSTON, on September 17, 1861, sent General S. B. Buckner, who had left Kentucky and entered the Confederate service, to seize and occupy Bowling Green, in Kentucky, with a force of 4,000 men. Bowling Green is at the crossing of the Big Barren River by the Louisville and Nashville road. A little to the south the Memphis and Ohio branches off from the Louisville and Nashville. Bowling Green was therefore a gateway through which all approach to the south from Louisville by rail must pass. There was no access by rail from the Ohio River to the south, east of Bowling Green. The road from Paducah led nowhere. The railroads to the north from Mississippi ended, not on the Ohio, but at Columbus, on the Mississippi. Defensive earthworks had already been begun at Fort Donelson, on the left Bank of the Cumberland, Fort Henry, on the right bank of the Tennessee, twelve miles west of Fort Donelson, and at Columbus, on the Mississippi. General Johnston, with the aid of his engineers, Lieutenant Dixon and Major J. F. Gilmer, afterward General and Chief Engineer of the Confederate army, adopted these sites as places to be strongly fortified. The line from Columbus to Bowling Green became the line chosen to bar access from the North to the South, and to serve as a base for invasion of the North.

The idea of breaking this line by an expedition up the

Tennessee and Cumberland Rivers seems to have presented itself to many. Colonel Charles Whittlesy, of the Twentieth Ohio, a graduate of West Point and formerly in the army, while acting as Chief Engineer on the staff of General O. M. Mitchell in Cincinnati, wrote to General Halleck, November

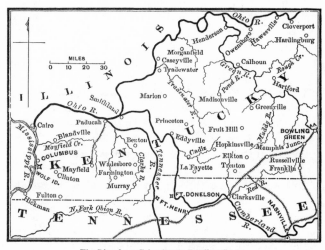

The Line from Columbus to Bowling Green.

20, 1861, suggesting a great movement by land and water up the Cumberland and Tennessee Rivers, on the ground that this was the most feasible route into Tennessee, and would necessitate the evacuation of Columbus and the retreat of Buckner from Bowling Green. In December, 1861, General Sherman, conversing with General Halleck, in St. Louis, suggested that the proper place to break the line was the centre, to which Halleck assented, pointing on the map to the Tennessee River, and saying that is the true line of

II.—2

operations. On January 3, 1862, General D. C. Buell, in a
letter to General Halleck, proposed a combined attack on
the centre and flanks of General Johnston's line, and added:
"The attack on the centre should be made by two gunboat
expeditions, with, I should say, 20,000 men on the two
rivers." General Halleck, writing to General McClellan,
January 20, 1862, said a movement down the Mississippi was
premature; that a more feasible plan was to move up the
Cumberland and Tennessee, making Nashville the objective
point, which movement would threaten Columbus and force
the abandonment of Bowling Green, adding "but the plan
should not be attempted without a large force—not less than
60,000 men." General McClellan, however, thought such
a movement should be postponed for the present. He wrote
on January 6th, to General Buell, Commander of the Department of the Ohio, which department included all of Kentucky east of the Cumberland River: "My own general plans
for the prosecution of the war make the speedy occupation
of East Tennessee and its lines of railway matters of absolute
necessity. Bowling Green and Nashville are in that connection of very secondary importance at the present moment."
General Grant wrote no reasoned speculations about it, but
throughout January pressed Halleck for permission to make
the attempt.

On January 6, 1862, Grant wrote to General Halleck for
permission to visit St. Louis. On the same day General
Halleck, in pursuance of orders received from General Mc-
Clellan, who was then in Washington in supreme command
of the United States forces, directed General Grant to make
a demonstration on Mayfield, in the direction of Murray. He
was directed to "make a great fuss about moving all your
force toward Nashville," and let it be understood that twenty
or thirty thousand men are expected from Missouri. He was

further directed to give this out to the newspapers, ana not let his own men or even his staff know the contrary. At the same-time he was advised that the real object was to prevent reinforcements being sent to Buckner, and charged not to advance far enough to expose his flank or rear to an attack from Columbus, and by all means to avoid a serious engagement. On the 10th, Halleck telegraphed to delay ; but Grant was already gone, with McClernand and 6,000 men from Cairo and Bird's Point, and had sent General C. F. Smith from Paducah with two brigades. The troops were out more than a week. The weather was cold, with rain and snow. The excursion was good practice in campaigning for the new volunteers, and detained reinforcements at Columbus while General George H. Thomas fought and won the battle of Mill Springs, in Kentucky.

General Grant, on his return to Cairo, wrote again on January 20th for permission to visit St. Louis. Receiving General Smith's report on the 22d, in which Smith said that the capture of Fort Henry was feasible—that two guns would make short work of it, he at once forwarded the report to St. Louis, and on the same day obtained the permission sought. When he began to unfold the object of his visit, to obtain permission to capture Henry and Donelson, Halleck silenced him so quickly and sharply that he said no more, and returned to Cairo believing his commander thought him guilty of proposing a military blunder. But, persisting still, he telegraphed on the 28th that, if permitted, he would take Fort Henry and establish and hold a camp there. Next day he wrote to the same effect in detail. On the 28th, Commodore A. H. Foote, flag-officer of the gunboat fleet, wrote to General Halleck that he concurred with General Grant, and asking if they had Halleck's authority to move when ready. On January 30th, General Halleck telegraphed to Grant to get ready, and made an order directing him to proceed. The order was received on February 1st, and next day General Grant started up the Tennessee with 17,000 men on transports, convoyed by Commodore Foote with seven gunboats.

The sites of Forts Henry and Donelson were chosen, and the work of fortifying them begun, by the State of Tennessee, when Kentucky was still holding itself neutral. Fort Donelson, immediately below the town of Dover, was a good position, and was near the Kentucky line. The site chosen for Fort Henry commanded a straight stretch of the river for some miles, and was near the State line and near Donelson. But it was low ground, commanded by higher ground on both sides of the river, and was washed by high water. Under the supervision of General A. S. Johnston's engineers, the work had become a well-traced, solidly constructed fortification of earth, with five bastions mounting twelve guns, facing the river, and five guns bearing upon the land. Infantry intrenchments were thrown up on the nearest high land, extending to the river both above and below the main work, and commanding the road to Fort Donelson. A work named Fort Heiman was begun on the bluff on the opposite side of the river, but was incomplete.

General McClernand, commanding the advance, landed eight miles below the fort. General Grant made a reconnoissance in one of the gunboats to draw the fire of the fort and ascertain the range of its guns. Having accomplished this, he re-embarked the landed troops, and debarked on February 4th, at Bailey's Ferry, three miles below the fort and just out of range of its fire. The river overflowed its banks, much of the country was under water; a heavy rain fell. The entire command did not get ashore till in the night of the 5th. In the night, General C. F. Smith was sent across the river to take Fort Heiman, but it was evacuated while Grant was landing his force at Bailey's Ferry. McClernand was ordered to move out at eleven o'clock in

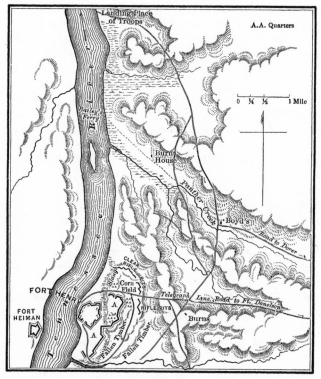

Fort Henry.

the morning of the 6th, and take position on the roads to Fort Donelson and Dover.

General Tilghman had telegraphed for reinforcements,

and had about thirty-four hundred men with him, but only one company of artillerists. At midnight of the 5th he telegraphed to General A. S. Johnston that Grant was intrenching at Bailey's Ferry. But, on the morning of the 6th, Tilghman gave up the idea of using his infantry in the defence, ordered Colonel Heiman to move the command to Fort Donelson, while he remained with the company of artillerists to engage the fleet and the land force, if it should appear, with the heavy armament of the fort, and thus retard pursuit.

At eleven o'clock in the morning of the 6th, General Grant moved with his command, and at the same time Commodore Foote steamed up the river with his fleet in two divisions. The first was of ironclads, the Cincinnati, flag-ship, the Carondelet, and the St. Louis, each carrying thirteen guns, and the Essex, carrying nine guns. The second division of three wooden boats, under command of Lieutenant Phelps, followed half a mile astern. At a quarter before twelve o'clock the first division opened fire with their bow-guns at a distance of seventeen hundred yards, and continued firing while slowly advancing to a distance of six hundred yards from the fort. Here the four boats took position abreast, and fired with rapidity. Lieutenant Phelps' division sent shells falling within the work. The little garrison replied with spirit. Fifty-nine shots from their guns struck the fleet, but most of them rebounded without doing harm. One shot exploded the boiler of the Essex, scalding twenty-eight officers and seamen, including Commander Porter. One seaman was killed and nine wounded on the flag-ship, and one was killed by a ball on the Essex. In the fort, the twenty-four pound rifled gun exploded, disabling every man at the piece; a shell from the fleet, exploding at the mouth of one of the thirty-two pounders, ruined the gun, and killed or wounded all the men serving it. A premature explosion at a forty-two pounder killed three men and wounded others. A priming-wire accidentally spiked the ten-inch columbiad. Five men were killed, eleven wounded, and five missing. Four guns were disabled. The men were discouraged. General Tilghman took personal charge of one of the guns and worked it, but he could no longer inspirit his men. Colonel Gilmer, Chief Engineer of the Department, and a few others, not willing to be included in the surrender, left the fort and proceeded to Fort Donelson on foot. At five minutes before two o'clock General Tilghman lowered his flag, and sent his adjutant by boat to report to the flag-officer of the fleet. Twelve officers and sixty-six men in the fort, and sixteen men in the hospital-boat, surrendered. Flag-officer Foote, in his report, says the hospital-boat contained sixty invalids. All the camp-equipage and stores of the force that retreated to Fort Donelson were included in the surrender; the troops, having no wagons, had left everything behind.

At eleven o'clock, General McClernand moved out with his division, followed by the third brigade of General C. F. Smith's division. McClernand had two brigades, the first commanded by Colonel R. J. Oglesby, the second by Colonel W. H. L. Wallace. With each brigade were two batteries —Schwartz and Dresser with the first brigade, Taylor and McAlister with the second. The order to McClernand was to take position on the road from Fort Henry to Fort Donelson and Dover, prevent all reinforcements to Fort Henry or escape from it, and be in readiness to charge and take Fort Henry by storm promptly on the receipt of orders. The road was everywhere miry, owing to the wet season, and crossed ridges and wet hollows. McClernand reports that the distance by road, from the camp to the fort, was eight miles. The troops, pulling through the mud, cheered the bombardment by the fleet when it opened. At three o'clock McClernand learned that the enemy were evacuating the fort, and ordered his cavalry to advance if the report was found to be true. Captain Stewart, of McClernand's staff, came upon the rear of the retiring force just as they were leaving the outer line of the earthworks. Colonel Dickey, of the Fourth Illinois cavalry, coming up, pursued the retreating column three miles, capturing 38 prisoners, six pieces of artillery, and a caisson. The head of the infantry column entered the fort at half-past three o'clock.

Commodore Foote turned over the prisoners and captured property to General Grant, sent Lieutenant Phelps with the wooden gunboats on an expedition up the Tennessee, and returned the same evening to Cairo with two gunboats. Lieutenant-Commander Phelps proceeded up the river to Florence, at the foot of the Muscle Shoals, in the State of Alabama. An account of this expedition and its brilliant success belongs to the naval history of the war.

CHAPTER III.

FORT DONELSON.

THE capture of Fort Henry was important, but it would be of restricted use unless Fort Donelson should also be taken. At this point the Cumberland and Tennessee Rivers are only twelve miles apart. The little town of Dover stood upon a bluff on the left bank of the Cumberland. Immediately above it, two small brooks empty into the river, making a valley or bottom overflowed by every high water. Immediately below the town is Indian Creek. One branch of it, rising close by the head of the upper one of the two brooks, flowing outwardly from the river toward the west, then bending to the north and northeast, makes almost the circuit of the town, about half a mile from it, before emptying into the creek. Several small brooks, flowing from the north into Indian Creek, make deep ravines, which leave a series of ridges, very irregular in outline, but generally parallel to the river. About half a mile below the mouth of Indian Creek, Hickman Creek, flowing eastwardly, empties into the river at right angles with it. Small branches running into Hickman Creek almost interlock with those emptying into Indian Creek, whereby the series of ridges parallel to the river are made to extend continuously from the valley of one creek to the valley of the other.

Fort Donelson, a bastioned earthwork, was erected on the river-bluff, between the two creeks, its elevation being one

hundred feet above the water. A bend in the river gives
the fort command over it as far as its armament could carry.
On the slope of the ridge facing down stream, two water-
batteries were excavated. The lower battery and larger one,
was so excavated as to leave traverses between the guns. A
ten-inch columbiad and nine thirty-two pound guns constituted the armament of the lower battery; a rifled piece,
carrying a conical ball of one hundred and twenty-eight
pounds, with two thirty-two pound carronades, the armament of the upper. These water-batteries were, according
to Colonel J. D. Webster, General Grant's chief of staff,
thirty feet above the water-level at the time of the attack.
Colonel Gilmer, the engineer who constructed them, reported them as being fifty feet above the water-level; but
it does not appear at what stage of the water. As the narrow channel of the river allowed an attacking party to present only a narrow front, the batteries required but little
horizontal range for their guns, and the embrasures were
accordingly made quite narrow. Eight additional guns were
in the fort.

Colonel Gilmer, going from Fort Henry to Fort Donelson,
immediately began the tracing and construction of works for
infantry defence. The river protected the east face of the
position, and the valley of Hickman Creek, filled with back-
water from the river, sufficiently guarded the north. The
line traced was two miles and a half long, following the re-
cessions and salients. The right of the line, occupying a
ridge extending from creek to creek, was nearly parallel
with the river, and distant from it fourteen hundred yards
in an air-line. It was somewhat convex, projecting to the
front about its centre, at the point where Porter's battery was
afterward posted. The left, facing to the south and southwest, beginning just above Dover, on the point of a ridge

extending nearly to the river between the two small brooks, continued out from the river along this ridge to its western extremity, and thence across the valley of the small curved

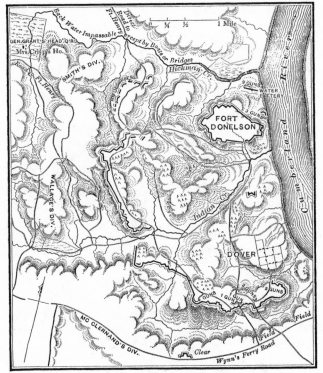

Fort Donelson.

stream described as encircling Dover and emptying into Indian Creek, to a V-shaped eminence in the fork between this small stream and Indian Creek. This salient termination was on the continuation of the line of the right or the west face of the infantry works. This point was assigned to Maney's battery and Heiman's brigade. The line of infantry defence was what came to be called, during the war, rifle-pit—a trench with the earth thrown up on the outer side. Batteries were constructed at nine points in the line, and armed with the guns of eight field batteries.

The valley of Indian Creek made a break in the line ; there was an interval at the creek between the portion occupied by Heiman's line and the work on the opposite slope, afterward the extreme left of General Buckner's command. The entire line on both faces, except the portion crossing the small valley or ravine to Heiman's left, followed the face of ridges from fifty to eighty feet high, faced by valleys or ravines filled with forest and underbrush. The trees were cut about breast-high, and the tops bent over outward, forming a rude abattis extremely difficult to pass through. The back-water filling the valley of Hickman Creek was an advantage to the defenders of Donelson, in so far as it served as a protection to one face of the position, and diminished the distance to be guarded and fortified. It was quite as great an advantage to the besiegers as it was to the besieged. They were by it relieved from a longer, being an exterior, line. Their transports and supplies could be landed and hauled out in security. Moreover, the back-water extending up Indian Creek also, within the defensive lines, cut the position in two, and made communication between the two parts inconvenient.

Immediately upon the capture of Fort Henry, work was begun on this line of infantry defence. The garrison, increased by the force from Fort Henry, numbered about six thousand effective men, under the command of Brigadier-General Bushrod R. Johnson. General Pillow, ordered by

General A. S. Johnston, arrived on February 9th from Clarksville with 2,000 men. He was immediately followed by General Clarke, who had been stationed at Hopkinsville with 2,000 more; and Generals Floyd and Buckner, who were at Russellville with 8,000 more, followed. General Johnston began to set them all in motion by telegram from Bowling Green, before he received news of the surrender of Fort Henry. General Floyd was so averse to going to Donelson that he continued to remonstrate. General Buckner, whose division had arrived, proposed on the night of the 11th to take it back to General Floyd, his commanding officer at Clarksville; but Pillow, who was senior to Buckner, ordered him to remain, and repaired himself to Clarksville. Under the combined influence of Pillow's persuasion and General Johnston's orders, Floyd finally made up his mind to go, and arrived at Donelson with the last of his command in the night of the 12th. Meanwhile, Major-General Polk had sent 1,860 men from Columbus. On the night of February 12th, Donelson was defended by about 20,000 men. The heavy guns in the water batteries were manned mostly by details from light batteries and artillery drilled a short time before the national force appeared, by two artillery officers, under the supervision of Colonel Milton A. Haynes, Chief of the Tennessee Corps of Artillery.

General Grant, in reporting to General Halleck, on February 6th, the surrender of Fort Henry, added: "I shall take and destroy Fort Donelson on the 8th, and return to Fort Henry." It was soon clear that he could not haul wagons over the road, and he proposed to go without wagons and double-team his artillery. The water continued rising. For two miles inland from Fort Henry the road was for the greater part under water. On the 8th he telegraphed: "I contemplated taking Fort Donelson to-day with infantry and cavalry alone, but all my troops may be kept busily engaged in saving what we now have from the rapidly rising water." The cavalry, however, fording the overflow, went to the front of Donelson on the 7th, skirmished with the pickets, and felt the outposts.

General Halleck went earnestly to work gathering and forwarding troops and supplies. Seasoned troops from Missouri, and regiments from the depots in Illinois, Indiana, and Ohio—so freshly formed that they had hardly changed their civil garb for soldier's uniform before they were hurried to the front to take their first military lessons in the school of bivouac and battle—were alike gathered up. General Halleck telegraphed Grant to use every effort to transform Fort Henry into a work strong on its landward side, and by all means to destroy the railroad bridge across the Cumberland at Clarksville, above Fort Donelson. Grant was urging Commodore Foote to send boats up the Cumberland to co-operate in an attack on Donelson.

On February 11th, Foote sailed from Cairo with his fleet. On the same day Grant sent six regiments, which had arrived at Fort Henry on transports, down the river on the boats from which they had not landed, to follow the fleet up the Cumberland. He also on the same day moved the greater part of his force out several miles from Fort Henry on to solid ground. On the morning of the 12th, leaving General L. Wallace and 2,500 men at Fort Henry, he moved by two roads, diverging at Fort Henry, but coming together again at Dover, with 15,000 men and eight field batteries. The force was organized in two divisions; the first commanded by General McClernand, the second by General C. F. Smith. McClernand had three brigades. The first, commanded by Colonel R. J. Oglesby, comprised the Eighth, Eighteenth, Twenty-ninth, Thirtieth, and Thirty-first Illinois, the batteries of Schwartz and Dresser, and four companies of cavalry. The second, commanded by Colonel W. H. L. Wallace, consisted of the Eleventh, Twentieth, Forty-fifth, and Forty-eighth Illinois, Colonel Dickey's Fourth Illinois Cavalry, and Taylor's and McAllister's batteries. The third, commanded by Colonel W. R. Morrison, comprised the Seventeenth and Forty-ninth Illinois. Smith's first brigade, commanded by Colonel John McArthur, was composed of the Ninth, Twelfth, and Forty-first Illinois. The second brigade was left at Fort Henry. The third, Colonel John Cook, contained the Fifty-second Indiana, Seventh and Fiftieth Illinois, Thirteenth Missouri, and Twelfth Iowa; and the fourth, Colonel John G. Lauman, contained the Twenty-fifth and Fifty-sixth Indiana, and the Second, Seventh, and Fourteenth Iowa. Major Cavender's battalion of Missouri artillery was attached to the division. Some of Major Cavender's guns were twenty-pounders. Three pieces in McAllister's battery were twenty-four pound howitzers.

McClernand's division, preceded by the Fourth Illinois cavalry, marched in advance on both roads. No opposition was encountered before reaching the pickets in front of Donelson. The advance came in sight of the fort about noon. McArthur's brigade, forming the rear of the column, halted about three miles from the fort at 6 P.M., and moved into position at half-past ten. It was observed by Colonel W. H. L. Wallace, whose brigade was at the head of the column on the telegraph or direct road between Forts Henry and Donelson, that the enemy's camps were on the other side of the creek, which, on examination, was found to be impassable. He moved up the creek and joined Colonel Oglesby, whose brigade was the advance on the Ridge road, in a wooded hollow, screened from view from the works by an intervening ridge.

The moment that deployment was begun, Oglesby's brig-

ade, which was the farther to the right, was briskly attacked by cavalry, who, after a sharp skirmish, retired.
McClernand's division was assigned to the right, C. F.
Smith's to the left. The day was spent feeling through the
thick woods and along deep ravines, and high, narrow
winding ridges. At times a distant glimpse was caught,
through some opening, of the gleam of tents crowning a
height; at times, a regiment tearing its way through blind-
ing undergrowth was startled and cut by the sudden discharge from a battery almost overhead, which it had come
upon unawares. The advancing skirmish-line was in constant desultory conflict with the posted picket-line. Batteries, occasionally, where an opening through the timber
permitted, took a temporary position and engaged the hostile batteries. The afternoon passed in thus developing the
fire of the line of works, feeling towards a position and
acquiring an idea of the formation of the ground. Smith's
division, by night, was in line in front of Buckner, and
McClernand's right had crossed Indian Creek and reached
the Wynn's Creek road. The column had marched without
transportation. The men had nothing but what they carried
in knapsack and haversack. Shelter-tents had not yet come
into use. The danger of drawing the enemy's fire prevented
the lighting of camp-fires. The army bivouacked in line of
battle. The besieged resumed at night their task, which
had been interrupted by the afternoon skirmishing, of completing and strengthening their works.

Next morning, Thursday the 13th, arrived, and the fleet
had not come. Fifteen thousand men, without supplies, confronted 20,000 well intrenched. A party was sent to destroy
the railroad bridge over the Tennessee, above Fort Henry,
the trestle approach to which had been partly destroyed by
Lieutenant-Commander Phelps, to prevent effectually rein-

forcements reaching Donelson from Columbus. Order was
sent to General Lewis Wallace, who had been left with a
brigade in command at Fort Henry, to join the besieging
force. The two divisions on the ground prosecuted the
work of feeling for position and probing the enemy. Colonel
Lauman's brigade, of C. F. Smith's division, bivouacked the
night of the 12th, about a mile from the intrenchments. On
the 13th he moved over the intervening ridges till he came
in view of the portion of the works held by Colonel Hanson,
constituting the right of General Buckner's line. A deep
hollow filled with timber filled the space between Lauman
and the works before him. On the farther slope, crowned
by the works, the slashed timber made an extensive abattis.
Colonel Veatch, with the Twenty-fifth Indiana, advanced
across the ravine or hollow, and forced his way partly up
the slope. He remained with his command two hours exposed to a fire to which, from their position, they could
make no effectual reply, and were recalled. The Seventh
and Fourteenth Iowa moved up to the left of the position
reached by Colonel Veatch, and a detachment of sharpshooters was posted so as to reach with their fire the men in
the trenches and divert their fire. At night Lauman withdrew his command to the place of the previous night's bivouac.
Colonel Cook's brigade advanced, the morning of the 13th, on
the right of Lauman's. The left of his line came also in front
of Hanson's works. The valley was here filled with such an
"immensity of abattis" that he did not feel justified in ordering an attempt to cross it, but kept up through the day
a desultory fire of skirmishers and sharpshooters over it.
The demonstration made by Lauman and Cook appeared
so threatening that General Buckner sent the Eighteenth
Tennessee to reinforce Hanson. The Seventh Illinois, which
constituted the right of Cook's advance moving through the

timber where a ridge leads to a battery at a salient in General Buckner's line, suddenly found itself under fire and retired. Colonel Cook formed his line with the other four regiments upon a ridge overlooking the enemy's intrenchments, about six hundred yards from them, separated from them by a valley dense with timber, mostly cut so as to form abattis, and remained in this position for the night.

McClernand continued pressing all day to his right, following the course of the ridge along which the Wynn's Ferry road passes. By night his right nearly or quite reached the point where the Wynn's Ferry road issued from the intrenchments. His artillery was very active ; the companies acting at times separately, at times uniting and concentrating their fire on some well-served battery, they silenced temporarily several batteries, and in the afternoon shelled some camps. A determined assault was made on the position held by Maney's battery, supported by Colonel Heiman with the Tenth, Forty-eighth, and Fifty-third Tennessee, and the Twenty-seventh Alabama. This position was, at the same time, the most salient and the most elevated in the entire line of intrenchment. It was so traced that both faces were swept by artillery and infantry fire from portions of the works to the right and the left. Colonel Morrison was directed with his brigade, the Seventeenth and Forty-ninth Illinois, to assault this position. Colonel Haynie, of the Forty-eighth Illinois, senior to Morrison, was ordered to join him and take the command. Morrison, on the right, assaulted the left face of the work ; the Seventeenth and Twenty-fifth assaulted the right. Crossing the valley, they began the ascent, encountered the tangled abattis, and while striving to tear their way through it, under a plunging fire from the battery and the infantry above them, they were assailed by artillery and infantry from a long extent of line

beyond. They recoiled from this toil and this double fire.
The Forty-fifth Illinois was sent to reinforce Morrison. The
four regiments started again, forced their way still farther
up the abattis, and were again repelled. Undaunted, they
rushed up the hill-side the third time. Part of the command
pierced through the abattis and reached the rifle-pits. The
summit of the rifle-pits was a blaze of musketry. Maney's
guns hurled shrapnel into their faces. To Morrison's right
and to Haynie's left, the long line of rifle-pits was a line of
musketry, and from projecting points the batteries sent their
fire. Morrison was wounded. His men could not climb
over the intrenchment. The regiments recalled, fell back
in order out of fire. The dead leaves on the hill-side were
inflamed in some way, in this close contest, and when artillery and musketry had ceased, helpless wounded lying on
the hill-side were burned to death. Colonel Heiman's men,
leaping over their works, were able to save some. General
Buckner reported his loss in the assault on Hanson's position as thirty-nine killed and wounded. Ten killed and
thirty wounded were reported as Heiman's loss, most of them
in Maney's battery. Nearly every regiment in the entire
line of the intrenchments suffered some casualties from the
National artillery. The national loss was more severe. The
pertinacity of the attack through the day prevented the
besieged from suspecting the inferiority in numbers of the
attacking force.

The Carondelet, a thirteen-gun iron-clad, arrived in the
morning of the 13th, and fired at the water-batteries at long
range. One shot struck a thirty-two-pound gun, disabling
it, and killed Captain Dixon, of the engineers, who had assisted Colonel Gilmer in the construction of both Henry
and Donelson. A shot from the one hundred and twenty-
eight-pound gun in the upper battery, entering a port-hole,

damaged the machinery of the Carondelet, and she drew out
of range.

The fleet, together with transports bringing reinforcements and supplies, arrived toward evening. McClernand
had moved so far around to the right as to leave a wide gap
between his left and Smith's division. McArthur's brigade,
of Smith's division, was moved to the right. Near midnight,
upon the request of General McClernand, McArthur detached
two regiments and moved them farther to the right, to within
a quarter of a mile of McClernand's left. Severe wind set
in with the night. Snow fell and the ground froze. Fires
could not be lighted by either army. Some of McClernand's
regiments, having thrown away their blankets on going into
action, sat up all night.

General Lewis Wallace arrived from Fort Henry about
noon, Friday, the 14th, and was placed in command of a
division of troops just arrived on the transports, styled Third
Division. The First Brigade, commanded by Colonel Charles
Cruft, consisted of the Seventeenth and Twenty-fifth Kentucky, and the Thirty-first and Forty-fourth Indiana. The
Third Brigade, commanded by Colonel John M. Thayer,
comprised the Fifty-eighth and Seventy-sixth Ohio, and the
First Nebraska. The Second Brigade was not organized;
but in the course of Saturday, the Forty-sixth, Fifty-seventh,
and Fifty-eighth Illinois and Twentieth Ohio, reported separately, and were assigned to duty. General Wallace moved
into position on the right of General C. F. Smith, so as to
hold the narrow ridge or spur which faced the right of Buckner's line, and was separated from McClernand by the valley
of Indian Creek.

The day was quiet along the National lines, and was spent
in defining and adjusting the commands in position. Skirmishers exchanged occasional shots, and artillerists from

time to time tried the range of their guns. McClernand moved his right still nearer to the river, Oglesby's brigade reaching nearly to the extreme left of the Confederate works, and to the head of the back-water up the valley of the small brooks above Dover; the Eighth, Eighteenth, and Twenty-ninth Illinois were respectively posted across the three roads, which, leaving the main road along the ridge, called Wynn's Ferry road, crossed the hollow and through the enemy's intrenchments into Dover. The cavalry reconnoitered around the enemy's left, to the muddy and overflowed bottom extending back from the river immediately above Dover.

According to the report of General Buckner it was decided, in a council of general officers held that morning, to cut a way for the garrison out through the enclosing force at once, before delay would make it impracticable; that General Pillow was to lead, and Buckner to cover the retreat of the army if the sortie proved successful. Buckner made the necessary preparations, but early in the afternoon the order was countermanded by General Floyd, at the instance of General Pillow, who, after drawing out his troops for the attack, thought it too late for the attempt. Though this is not mentioned in the reports of General Floyd, General Pillow, or Colonel Gilmer, Colonel Baldwin in his report says that General Buckner formed his division in open ground to the left and rear of the intrenchments, for the purpose, apparently, of attacking the National right, Colonel Baldwin's command being the head of the column; that the column marched out by a road about two hundred yards from the left of the intrenchments, and approached the right of the National line by a course nearly perpendicular to it; but, after advancing a quarter of a mile, General Pillow said it was too late in the day to accomplish anything, and the troops returned to their quarters. Major Brown, commanding the Twentieth Mississippi, reports substantially the same, and adds they were under fire as soon as they began the advance, and one of his men was shot before they advanced one hundred yards.

About three o'clock in the afternoon Flag Officer Foote moved his fleet up the river to attack the fort. The flag-ship St. Louis and three other iron-clads, the Carondelet, Louisville, and Pittsburg, each armed with thirteen guns, advanced, followed by the wooden gunboats Tyler and Conestoga. The water-battery attacked was a mere trench twenty feet wide, sunk in the hill-side. The excavated earth thrown up outside the ditch made a rampart twelve feet through at the summit. Carefully laid sand-bags added to the height of the rampart, and left narrow spaces for embrasures; narrow, but sufficient there, where the channel of the river, straight and narrow, required the fleet to advance in a straight line and with a narrow front. Such a work, at an elevation of thirty feet above the water, was almost unassailable.

The gunboats opened fire when a mile and a half from the fort, and continued advancing slowly and firing rapidly till the ironclads were within four hundred yards of the battery. The boats could use only their bow-guns, three on each boat. After a severe action of an hour and a half, a solid shot entering the pilot-house of the flag-ship, carried away the wheel, and the tiller-ropes of the Louisville were disabled by a shot. The relieving-tackles being no longer able to steer or control these boats in the rapid current, they became wholly unmanageable, and drifted down the river. The other two boats were also damaged, and the whole fleet withdrew. There were fifty-four, officers and men, killed and wounded on the fleet—Commodore Foote being one of the wounded. The flag-ship alone was struck fifty-nine times. One rifled gun on the Carondelet burst during the action. The terrible pounding by the heavy navy guns seems to have inflicted no injury upon the earthworks, their armament, or the men.

Transports arrived in the course of the day, bringing additional reinforcements. General McArthur was ordered at 5 P.M. to occupy ground on the extreme right of the National line, to act as a reserve to General Oglesby. He reached the assigned position in the dark, about 7 P.M., and "encamped for the night, without instructions and without adequate knowledge of the nature of the ground in front and on the right." The troops, without shelter and without fires, suffered another night of cold and wind and snow and sleet, after a day without food.

In the night, General Floyd, in council with General Pillow, General Buckner, and Colonel Gilmer, determined to make a sortie in the morning, and, if practicable, cut a way out, and retreat by the Wynn's Ferry road to Charlotte. Pillow was to begin with an attack on McClernand's right, assisted by the cavalry. When he should succeed in pushing back the right, Buckner was to issue from the works and strike the division near its centre. When the whole of the division should be rolled back onto Lewis Wallace, leaving a cleared way out into the country over the road, Pillow's division was to lead, and Buckner to hold the National forces back and afterward serve as rear-guard on the retreat to Charlotte. The brigade commanders were sent for and received instructions. No instructions were given to them, nor was anything said in the council, as to what supplies the troops should carry, and some regiments took neither knapsacks nor rations. Before dawn, Saturday, the 15th, Pillow's division began assembling, as on the previous day, on open ground in rear of the extreme left of the intrenchments.

Colonel Baldwin, who was posted with two of his regiments, the Twenty-sixth Tennessee and Twenty-sixth Mississippi, in Pillow's portion of the intrenchments, while the rest of his brigade was west of Indian Creek, under Buckner, held the advance, the Twentieth Mississippi being added to his command, giving him a temporary brigade of three regiments. Colonel Heiman, with his brigade and Maney's battery, strengthed by the Forty-second Tennessee, were to remain in position and thence aid the attack while it was going on. The Thirtieth Tennessee was to occupy the trenches vacated by Buckner, while the Forty-ninth and Fiftieth Tennessee were to act as garrison to the main work—the fort.

Commodore Foote wrote to General Grant desiring an interview with him, and asking, as he was disabled by wounds, to be excused from going to see Grant, requested that the interview be held on the flag-ship. The Twentieth Ohio, which had arrived on transports the evening before and was ordered to report to General Lewis Wallace the day before, while marching after breakfast from the boats to the fort, met General Grant with some of his staff riding down the river road to where the boats lay. The sally had been made and the attack begun ; but there was nothing in the sound that came through several miles of intervening forest to indicate anything more serious than McClernand's previous assaults.

Baldwin's brigade, leaving the intrenchments at 6 A.M., marched by the right flank out a narrow and obstructed by-road, crossed the valley in front of the works, and, while ascending the slope beyond, encountered what they supposed to be a line of pickets. But Oglesby's hungry men had slept little that cold night, and by simply rising to their feet were in line of battle. Baldwin's brigade, in attempting to deploy, was thrown into confusion, repeatedly rallied, and was thrown into disorder and pushed back before its line was established. Colonel Baldwin, in his report, says that deployment forward into line would have brought his men into such an exposed situation that he threw his regiment first into column of company, then deployed on the right into line, and admits that practising tactics with new troops under fire is a different thing from practice on the drill-ground. The movement that Colonel Baldwin attempted with his leading regiment, the Twenty-sixth Mississippi, is the same that General Sigel accomplished at Pea Ridge with such brilliant effect, where he had by artillery fire to drive back the enemy's line to gain room for each successive deployment.

The firing sufficiently notified General McArthur where he was, and, without waiting for orders, he formed his brigade into line on Oglesby's right. Pillow's division, continually filing out from the intrenchments, continually extended his line to his left. McArthur, to gain distance to his right, widened the intervals between his regiments, refused his right, and prolonged it by a skirmish line. Oglesby brought into action Schwartz's battery, then commanded by Lieutenant Gumbart, and the batteries in position in the besieged intrenchments joined in the combat. A tenacious fight, face to face, ensued—so stationary that its termination seemed to be a mere question of endurance and ammunition. General Pillow moved the Twentieth Mississippi by wheeling its left to the front. In this position the regiment suffered so severely that it withdrew and took shelter behind a rising ground. A depression was found by which General B. R. Johnson's brigade could find comparative protection while moving to their left and gaining distance to their front. General McArthur found his right flank turned and his ammunition nearly exhausted, and withdrew his brigade

II.—3

to a new position several hundred yards to his rear. Oglesby moved the Eighteenth Illinois to the right, to partially fill the vacated line, and brought up the Thirtieth Illinois from its position in reserve to take the place left by the Eighteenth. Colonel Lawler, of the Eighteenth, was wounded early in the engagement. Captain Brush, who had succeeded to the command, was wounded while carrying out this movement. The ammunition of the Eighteenth being now nearly gone, it retired in good order to replenish, leaving 44 of its number dead, and 170 wounded on the ground where it had stood.

McClernand, when he found his command heavily pressed, sent to Lewis Wallace, the adjoining division commander, for aid. Wallace sent to Grant's headquarters for instructions, but the General was away on the flag-ship, and his staff did not take the responsibility of acting in his place. Wallace, having been ordered to act on the defensive, declined to move without first receiving an order. When McArthur fell back, Oglesby's right became enveloped, McClernand repeated his request, and Wallace, seeing the affair was serious, took the responsibility, and ordered Cruft's brigade to advance. The Twenty-fifth Kentucky, on coming up, by some mistake fired into the Eighth and Twenty-ninth Illinois. These regiments and the Thirtieth Illinois broke and retired. The Eighth had lost 55 killed and 188 wounded; the Twenty-ninth, 25 killed and 60 wounded; the Thirtieth, 19 killed and 71 wounded. The wounded had been taken off to a building in the rear, which was turned into a hospital. Cruft maintained his position stoutly, receiving and making charges, and firing steadily from line. His men found the same difficulty that is mentioned in reports of other commanders, of distinguishing the enemy except when close at hand, or in motion. Their uniform, of the same color with the dead leaves of dense scrub-oak, uniforms and foliage at a short distance were undistinguishable. McArthur drew his brigade back out of the contest, halted, and obtained ammunition and rations. His men, who had fasted thirty-six hours, had one good meal before they moved toward night to the extreme left, in support of the troops there engaged. Cruft's brigade, being isolated, finally retired to the right and rear, and took position near the hospital.

When the rest of Oglesby's brigade retreated, the Thirty-first Illinois, Colonel John A. Logan, the left of the brigade and connecting with the right of Colonel W. H. L. Wallace's brigade, wheeled so as to have its line at right angles with the line of the enemy's intrenchments; for, as McArthur's and Oglesby's commands crumbled away, Pillow's division, rolling up McClernand's, were now advancing in a course parallel to the front of their intrenchments. The Thirty-first held its ground; but yielding was only a question of time. As Pillow's division in deploying continually increased its front, Colonel Baldwin's brigade was continually pressed to his right and came in front of W. H. L. Wallace's brigade. McCausland's brigade, consisting of the Thirty-sixth and Fiftieth Virginia, formed on Baldwin's right and in front of W. H. L. Wallace. Their assault was aided by the batteries in position in the intrenchments, and Wallace's batteries alternately replied to the artillery and played upon the line of infantry. Wallace held his line, and Pillow sent to Buckner to advance. Buckner held his command within the intrenchments massed, waiting for his opportunity. He sent three regiments, Third Tennessee, Eighteenth Tennessee, and Fourteenth Mississippi, across the intervening hollow. They attacked with spirit; but, confused by the missiles flying overhead, broken by pushing through the

snow-covered boughs, and galled by the hot fire they encountered, they quickly fell back in disorder, and, according to General Buckner, communicated their depression to
the rest of his command.

Toward noon, as McClernand's right was rolled up and
began to crumble, Buckner, who had cheered his men, now
led his division farther to his right, near to Heiman's position in the intrenchments; there he approached under
cover till near Wallace's line.   Three batteries supported
his charge—Maney's, Porter's, and Graves', these three batteries concentrating their fire on Wallace's artillery.   Forrest brought his cavalry forward.   Wallace's brigade, with
Taylor's and McAllister's batteries, and Logan's regiment,
with boxes nearly empty, withstood the combined attack.
McAllister fired his last round of ammunition.   Taylor had
fired seventeen hundred rounds of ammunition, an average
of two hundred and eighty-three rounds to the piece.   The
infantry fired their last cartridge.   The batteries of Maney,
Graves, and Porter poured in their fire ; the divisions of Pillow and Buckner aided—some regiments at a halt firing, but
Buckner's advancing.   Forrest's cavalry hovered on the outskirts.   Wallace gave the command to fall back.   McAllister
had not horses left to haul off his three howitzers, and had
to leave two.   The order did not reach the Eleventh Illinois.
The rest of the command fell back in regular order, and the
Eleventh and Thirty-first continued fighting.   Colonel Logan, of the Thirty-first, was wounded ; the lieutenant-colonel
was killed.   Thirty others were killed.   The ranks were
thinned by the wounded who had fallen and been carried
off the field.   Ammunition was gone.   Logan told Lieutenant-Colonel Ransom, of the Eleventh Illinois, who, having
had his wound dressed, had returned to his regiment, that
the Thirty-first must leave, and suggested that the Eleventh

should take the position left by the Thirty-first. The Thirty-first marched steadily from the field, and the Eleventh, alone now, faced to the rear, wheeled to the left, and continued the fight. But, assailed on both flanks as well as in front, and finally charged by the cavalry, it was broken, and fell back in disorder. The brigade fell back half a mile.

Fugitives from the front passed by General Lewis Wallace, who was conversing with Captain Rawlins, General Grant's assistant adjutant-general. Among them a mounted officer galloped down the road, shouting, "We are cut to pieces." General Wallace at once ordered Colonel Thayer's brigade to the front. Marching by the flank, they soon met portions of Oglesby's and Colonel Wallace's brigades retiring from the field. They all stated they were out of ammunition. Thayer's brigade passed on at a double-quick. Position was taken ; a battery, Company A, Chicago Light Artillery, commanded by Captain Wood, was posted across the road ; to its right, the First Nebraska and Fifty-eighth Illinois ; to the left, the Fifty-eighth Ohio and a company of the Thirty-second Illinois. The Seventy-sixth Ohio and Forty-sixth and Fifty-seventh Illinois were posted in reserve. As soon as this line was formed, interposed between the enemy and the retiring regiments, they halted and waited for ammunition. The line was scarcely formed before a force, coming up the road and through the forest, made a fierce attack. The assault was vigorous. The line remained steady, and, with fire deliberate and well aimed, quickly drove off the assailants. That closed the attack made by the sortie. Colonel Cruft's brigade, the position of which was not then known to General Wallace, was off at the right, near enough to see the repulsed force retire in the direction of the works. Cruft's brigade was brought into alignment with Thayer's, and Wallace held the ground with his division.

McClernand's division was swept from the ground which it had occupied. The desired road for retreat was open to the besieged. Buckner was in the position assigned to him, and halting, awaited his artillery and reserves from the intrenchments. General Pillow, who now found himself within the intrenchments at the salient, held by Colonel Heiman, directed the artillery to remain, and sent reiterated orders to Buckner to return and resume his position within the works. He was in the act of returning when he met General Floyd, who seemed surprised at the movement. After some conversation, in which both agreed that the original plan should be carried out, Floyd directed Buckner to remain till he could see Pillow. After consulting with Pillow, Floyd sent orders to Buckner to retire within the lines, and to repair as rapidly as possible to his former position on the extreme right, which was in danger of attack. By order of General B. R. Johnson, Colonel Drake's brigade and the Twentieth Mississippi remained on the field.

General Grant, at his interview on the flag-ship, was advised of the serious injury to the fleet, and informed that Commodore Foote, leaving his two ironclads least injured to protect the transports at the landing, would proceed to Cairo with the other two, repair them, hasten the completion of the Benton and mortar-boats, and return to the prosecution of the siege. General Grant, upon this, made up his mind to intrench, and with reinforcements complete the investment of the enemy's works. Reaching the lines about one o'clock on his return, he learned the state of affairs, ordered General C. F. Smith to prepare to storm the works in his front, repaired to the right, inspected the condition of the troops, and gave orders to be ready to attack when General Smith should make his assault.

The Fifty-second Indiana had been detached from Colonel

Cook's brigade to watch a gap in the intrenchments, near the extreme right of the besieged line. At two o'clock General Smith ordered the assault by Lauman's brigade; the Fifty-second Indiana was temporarily attached to the brigade. The assaulting force was formed in column of battalions of five companies each. The Second Iowa was in advance, with General Smith in its centre, and followed in order by the Fifty-second Indiana, Twenty-fifth Indiana, Seventh Iowa, and Fourteenth Iowa. Birge's sharpshooters, deployed on each flank, opened a skirmishing fire. The column advanced silently, without firing, crushed down the abattis, covered the hill-side with battalions, heedless of the fire from the garrison, pressed on to the works, leaped over, formed in line, and drove the defending regiment to further shelter.

Just at this time General Buckner was gaining this, the extreme right of the line of intrenchments, with Hanson's regiment, which had left it in the morning for the sortie. Hanson pushed his men forward, but the works were occupied. The Thirtieth Tennessee, which had been holding that portion of the works during the day, fell back to another ridge or spur, between the captured work and the main fort. Lauman's brigade pushed on to assault that position. Hanson's regiment, the Third, Eighteenth, and Forty-first Tennessee and Fourteenth Mississippi, came to the aid of the Thirtieth; portions of Porter's and Graves' batteries were brought up. The Forty-ninth and Fiftieth Tennessee, the garrison of the fort, hastened out in support. General Smith sent for Cook's brigade and artillery. Lieutenant-Colonel McPherson sent up two ten-pound Parrott guns. Buckner held the inner ridge, to which his men had retired, and intrenched it in the night. Smith held the works he had gained, an elevation as high as any within the line. His

battery established there, enfiladed part of the line still
held, and took in reverse nearly the whole of the intrenchments. In the charge, the column, including Birge's sharpshooters, but excluding the Fifty-second Indiana, lost 61
killed and 321 wounded; of these, the Second Iowa lost
41 killed and 157 wounded. General Smith, though sixty
years old, spent the night without shelter, on the captured
ridge.

General Grant, having set in motion C. F. Smith's attack,
rode to the right and ordered the troops there to take the
offensive and regain the ground that had been lost. General Lewis Wallace moved with a brigade commanded by
Colonel Morgan L. Smith, and made of the Eighth Missouri
and Eleventh Indiana, in advance. These two regiments
belonged to Smith's division, and marched from Fort Henry
to Donelson with Wallace. Colonel M. L. Smith, in his report, calls this command the Fifth Brigade, Third Division.
The regimental commanders in their reports style it, Fifth
Brigade, General C. F. Smith's division. Following was
Cruft's brigade. General Wallace says, in his report: "As
a support, two Ohio regiments, under Colonel Ross, were
moved up and well advanced on the left flank of the assail-
ing force, but held in reserve." Colonel Ross, of the Seventeenth Illinois, arriving at the front that morning and
reporting for duty, was at once assigned to the command of
the brigade composed of the Seventeenth and Forty-ninth
Illinois, and, as ordered by General McClernand, moved with
General Wallace in support and reserve, till recalled about
dark by McClernand. An Ohio regiment, the Twentieth,
Colonel Whittlesey, did go out in support and reserve, but
it was not under Colonel Ross, and it remained close to the
enemy's works all night.

The column approached the ridge held by Drake's bri-

gade and the Twentieth Mississippi.   M. L. Smith's brigade
came in front, where the slope was bare ; Cruft had to push
up through bushes.   General Wallace speaks with admiration of the advance by Smith.   He advanced his line and
ordered it to lie down, and to continue firing while lying
down.   As soon as the fire of the enemy on the summit
slackened, the regiments rose, dashed up the hill, and lay
down again before the fire from the hill-top could be made
effective.   In a short time, with rapid bounds, the summit
was gained.   Cruft's brigade pushed up through the bushes.
Drake fell back within the intrenchments.   Wallace stationed his picket-line close to the enemy's works.   The retiring Confederate force took with them six captured pieces
of artillery, several thousand small arms, and between two
and three hundred prisoners ; but returned to their trenches
weary, disappointed, disheartened.

   In the night General Floyd and General Buckner met with
General Pillow and his staff, at General Pillow's headquarters, to consider the situation.   After some recrimination
between Pillow and Buckner whether the intention and plan
had been to commence the retreat directly from the battle-
field, or first to cut a way out and then return to the works,
equip for a march and retreat by night, it was agreed to
evacuate that night and march out by the ground which had
been gained.   Pillow ordered the chief quartermaster and
the chief commissary to burn the stores at half-past five
in the morning.   Precaution was taken, however, before actually preparing for the movement, to send out scouts to see
if the way were still clear.   The scouts returned with report that the National forces had reoccupied the ground.
This being doubted, other scouts were sent out, who brought
the same report in more positive terms.   Pillow proposed
to cut a way out.   Buckner said that was now impossible,

and Floyd acquiesced. Pillow at last assented to this, but proposed to hold the fort at least one day longer and take the chances of getting out. Buckner said that was impossible ; a lodgement had been made in the key of his position ; assault would certainly follow as soon as it was light, and he could not withstand it. It was remarked that no alternative was left but to surrender. General Floyd said he would never surrender—he would die first. Pillow said substantially the same. Buckner said, if he were in command, he would surrender and share the fate of the garrison. Floyd inquired of Buckner, "If the command should devolve on you, would you permit me to take out my brigade ?" To which Buckner replied, "Yes, if you leave before the terms of capitulation are agreed on." Forrest asked, "Gentlemen, have I leave to cut my way out ?" Pillow answered, "Yes, sir, cut your way out," and asked, "Is there anything wrong in my leaving ?" Floyd replied, "Every person must judge for himself of that ?" Whereupon General Pillow said, "Then I shall leave this place." General Floyd turned to General Pillow and told him, "General Pillow, I turn the command over, sir." General Pillow said, "And I pass it." General Buckner said, "And I assume it," and countermanded the order for the destruction of the commissary and quarter-master stores, and ordered white flags to be prepared and a bugler to report to him.

At eleven o'clock that night Floyd telegraphed to General A. S. Johnston a glorious victory. Four hours later, at the close of the council or conference, he telegraphed : "We are completely invested by an army many times our numbers. I regret to say the unanimous opinion of the officers seems to be that we cannot maintain ourselves against these forces."

Colonel Forrest reported that upon examination he found

that deep mud and water made an escape by land, between the investing force and the river, impracticable for infantry. Forrest marched out with all the cavalry but Gantt's Tennessee battalion and two companies of Helm's Kentucky cavalry, taking with him the horses of Porter's battery and about two hundred men of various commands. There was not a steamboat at the landing; General Floyd had sent all up the river with wounded and prisoners. Not a skiff or yawl could be found. A little flatboat or scow was got by some means from the other side of the river, and on this General Pillow crossed the river with his staff and Colonel Gilmer. Two steamboats returned at daybreak, one of them bringing "about four hundred raw troops." The four hundred raw troops were dumped on shore, and Floyd took possession of the boats. Floyd's brigade, consisting of four Virginia regiments and the Twentieth Mississippi, had been divided during the siege. The four Virginia regiments were organized into two brigades, and the Twentieth Mississippi attached to another command. Two Virginia regiments were ferried across the river, and the Twentieth Mississippi, understanding that they were to be taken on board with Floyd, stood on guard and kept off the growing crowd of clamorous soldiers while the other two Virginia regiments embarked. The rope was cut and Floyd steamed up the river, leaving the Twentieth Mississippi and his aid-de-camp, Lieutenant Breckenridge Drake, behind. It was said afterward that word was received from General Buckner that the boat must leave at once, or it would not be allowed to leave.

Soon after daybreak, Sunday the 16th, the men of Lauman's brigade heard the notes of a bugle advancing from the fort. It announced an officer, who bore to General Grant a letter from General Buckner, proposing the appointment of commissioners to agree upon terms of capitulation, and also proposing an armistice until noon. General Grant replied, acknowledging the receipt of the letter, and adding: "No terms except an unconditional and immediate surrender can be accepted. I propose to move immediately upon your works." Buckner replied: "The distribution of the forces under my command, incident to an unexpected change of commanders, and the overwhelming force under your command, compel me, notwithstanding the brilliant success of the Confederate arms yesterday, to accept the ungenerous and unchivalrous terms which you propose." White flags were displayed along the works; the National troops marched in, and General Grant at once made the following order: "All prisoners taken at the surrender of Fort Donelson will be collected as rapidly as practicable near the village of Dover, under their respective company and regimental commanders, or in such manner as may be deemed best by Brigadier-General S. B. Buckner, and will receive two days' rations preparatory to embarking for Cairo. Prisoners are to be allowed their clothing, blankets, and such private property as may be carried about the person, and commissioned officers will be allowed their side-arms."

There is disagreement as to the number of guns captured. There were thirteen in the water-batteries and eight in the fort. Besides, there were eight artillery companies, whose field-pieces were disposed in nine positions along the line of intrenchments. Six of these companies were those of Maney, Porter, Graves, Green, Guy, Jackson. The other two are called Ross and Murray in the account in the Nashville *Patriot*, and called Parker and French on the pen-sketch of the works showing the position of the light batteries, found among the Confederate records. The number of pieces in these batteries is not given. Badeau gives the number of guns surrendered at sixty-five, and no reason is seen why that is not correct.

There is no means of determining with any precision the number of the garrison. General Grant, on the day of the surrender, reported the number of prisoners taken as twelve to fifteen thousand. Badeau says the number captured was 14,623; and that rations were issued at Cairo to that number of prisoners taken at Fort Donelson. According to a report or estimate made by Major Johnson, of the first Mississippi, and found among his papers in Mississippi in 1864, the number "engaged" was 15,246, and the number surrendered 11,738. General Floyd gives no estimate. General Pillow, in his brief to the Secretary of War of the Confederacy, defending himself from charges, gives thirteen thousand as about the number engaged in the defence; while General Buckner, in a report made after he was exchanged, says the aggregate of the army within the works was never greater than twelve thousand. An estimate published in the Nashville *Patriot* soon after the surrender makes the number engaged 13,829.

Major Brown's estimate was evidently the most deliberate and careful, yet it is not free from error. It is not accurate in the number of casualties. The regimental reports made after the surrender are not numerous, but they present some means of testing Major Brown's estimate. According to that estimate, the Eighth Kentucky lost 19 killed and 41 wounded; according to the official report of Colonel Simonton, commanding the brigade, the loss of the Eighth Kentucky was 27 killed and 72 wounded. According to Major Brown's estimate, two of the Virginia regiments lost none killed or wounded, and the aggregate of the loss of the four regiments was 13 killed and 113 wounded; according to the brigade reports, every regiment lost both killed and wounded, the aggregate being 41 killed and 166 wounded. Major Brown's estimate omits the Kentucky cavalry bat-

talion of three companies. It names also only seven artillery companies, while the Nashville *Patriot's* account and the
memorandum on the manuscript plan of the intrenchments
name eight. This estimate is also incomplete. It gives
only the number engaged belonging to regiments and companies, and thereby excludes brigade and division commanders, and their staff and enlisted men at their headquarters;
it also excludes the "four hundred raw troops" (the reports
give them no other designation) who arrived too late to be
engaged, but in time to be surrendered; and the estimate
being only of those engaged, excludes sick, special duty
men, and all except the muskets and sabres present for duty
in the works. Such an estimate of "effective" or "engaged" is no basis for a statement of the number surrendered. The morning report of Colonel Bailey's regiment, the
Forty-ninth Tennessee, for January 14th, was 680 effectives
out of an aggregate of 777. His last morning report before
the surrender was 393 effectives out of an aggregate of 773.
Major Brown's estimate gives this regiment 372 engaged.
Colonel Bailey's morning report of those present with him
on the way from Donelson to Cairo, which included none
from hospitals, was, officers and men, 490.

There is no report of trustworthy accuracy, giving either
the aggregate or the effective strength. Ten thousand five
hundred prisoners were put into the charge of Colonel Whittlesey, of the Twentieth Ohio; of which number he sent north,
guarded by his own regiment, about six thousand three hundred; another, but much smaller body, was put into the hands
of Colonel Sweeney. Besides these, were the wounded and
sick in hospital, in camp, and some left on the field. Colonel Whittlesey, at the time, estimated the entire number
taken charge of, including sick and wounded, at 13,000.
General Floyd said that the boats which carried across and

up the river his four Virginia regiments, took at the same
time about as many other troops; and he says he took up
the river with him 986, officers and men, of the four Virginia regiments. Pillow reported, on March 14th, that several thousand infantry had got out in one way or other,
many of whom were at that time with him at Decatur, Ala.,
and the rest under orders to rendezvous there. They continued slipping out after the surrender. General B. R. Johnson, on the Tuesday after the surrender, not having reported
or been enrolled as a prisoner, walked with a fellow-officer
out of the intrenchments at mid-day, and, not being chal-
lenged, continued beyond the National camps and escaped.
The accounts of the escape by boat with Floyd, on horse
with Forrest, and by parties slipping out by day and by night
through the forest and undergrowth and the devious ravines, fairly show that 5,000 must have escaped. There was
scarcely a regiment or battery, if, indeed, there was a single regiment or battery, from which some did not escape.
Eleven hundred and thirty-four wounded were sent up the
river by boat the evening before the surrender, and General
Pillow estimated the killed at over four hundred and fifty.
This accounts for an aggregate of over nineteen thousand
five hundred, sufficiently near the estimate of nineteen thousand six hundred—the number in the place during the siege,
and the additional four hundred, who arrived only in time
to be surrendered.

General Floyd surmised the killed and wounded to be
fifteen hundred. Pillow estimated them at two thousand.
The National loss was, in McClernand's division, 1,445 killed
and wounded, and 74 missing; in C. F. Smith's division, 306
killed, 1,045 wounded, and 167 missing; and in Lewis Wallace's division, 39 killed, 248 wounded, and 5 missing—making an aggregate of 3,329 killed, wounded, and missing.

General Grant sat down before the place Wednesday the
12th, at noon, with 15,000 men, and with that number closed
in upon the works and made vigorous assaults next day.
Reinforcements began to arrive at the landing Thursday
evening, and when the place surrendered his army had
grown by reinforcements to twenty-seven thousand. Grant
had no artillery but the eight field-batteries which he brought
over from Fort Henry to Donelson. These were not fixed in
position and protected by earthworks, but were moved from
place to place and used as batteries in the field.

The defensive line from Columbus to Bowling Green,
broken by the capture of Fort Henry, was now shattered.
General A. S. Johnston evacuated Bowling Green on February 14th, and on the 17th and 18th moved with the main
body of his troops from Nashville to Murfreesboro. The
rear-guard left Nashville on the night of the 23d, and the
advance of Buell's army appeared next morning on the opposite bank of the river. Columbus was evacuated shortly
after. The National authority was re-established over the
whole of Kentucky, the State of Tennessee was opened to
the advance of both army and fleet, and the Mississippi was
cleared down to Island Number Ten.

General Halleck telegraphed on February 17th, the day
after the surrender, to General McClellan: "Make Buell,
Grant, and Pope major-generals of volunteers, and give
me command in the West. I ask this in return for Donelson and Henry." Next day, the 18th, he telegraphed to
General Hunter, commanding the Department of Kansas,
thanking him for his aid in sending troops; and to Grant,
ordering him not to let the gunboats go up higher than
Clarksville, whence they must return to Cairo immediately
upon the destruction of the bridge and railroad. On the
19th he telegraphed to Washington: "Smith, by his cool-

ness and bravery at Fort Donelson, when the battle was against us, turned the tide and carried the enemy's outworks. Make him a major-general. You cannot get a better one. Honor him for this victory, and the whole country will applaud." On the 20th he telegraphed to McClellan, "I must have command of the armies in the West. Hesitation and delay are losing us the golden opportunity." Upon the receipt in Washington of the news of the surrender of Fort Donelson, the President at once appointed Grant major-general, and the Senate immediately confirmed the appointment. Buell and Pope shortly after received the same promotion. Later, in March, C. F. Smith, McClernand, and Lewis Wallace were confirmed to the same rank. On March 11th, General Halleck was assigned to the command of the Department of the Mississippi, embracing all the troops west of a line drawn north and south indefinitely through Knoxville, Tenn., and east of the western boundary of Arkansas and Missouri. On February 15th, Grant had been assigned to the command of the Military District of Tennessee, the limits of which were not defined, and General W. T. Sherman succeeded to the command of the District of Cairo.

5

CHAPTER IV.

NEW MADRID AND ISLAND NUMBER TEN.

A DIVISION belonging to General Pope's command in Missouri went with General Curtis to Pea Ridge and Arkansas. A considerable portion of what was left was sent up the Tennessee and Cumberland to General Grant. On February 14, 1862, General Pope was summoned to St. Louis by General Halleck, and on the 18th General Halleck pointed out to him the situation at New Madrid and Island No. Ten, and directed him to organize and command a force for their reduction. On the 19th Pope left for Cairo to defend it from an attack then apprehended from Columbus. This apprehension being found to be groundless, he proceeded by steamboat, with a guard of 140 men, thirty miles up the river, and began at once to organize his expedition.

Major-General Polk, commanding at Columbus, having received instructions from the Confederate War Department, through General Beauregard, to evacuate Columbus and select a defensive position below, adopted that embracing Madrid Bend on the Tennessee shore, New Madrid on the Missouri shore, and Island No. Ten between them. The bluffs on the Missouri shore terminate abruptly at Commerce. Thence to Helena, Arkansas, the west bank of the Mississippi is everywhere low and flat, and in many places on the river, and to much greater extent a few miles back from the river, is a swamp. From Columbus to Fort Pillow, the Tennessee shore is of the same character. The river flowing almost due south for some miles to Madrid Bend, curves there to the west of north to New Madrid, and there making another bend, sweeps to the southeast and then nearly east, till, reaching Tiptonville, a point nearly due south of Madrid Bend, it turns again to the south. Island No. Ten begins at Madrid Bend and looks up the straight stretch of the river. From Island No. Eight, about four miles above Island No. Ten, the distance across the land to New Madrid is six miles, while by river it is fifteen. The distance overland from Island No. Ten to Tiptonville is five miles, while by water it is twenty-seven. Commencing at Hickman, between Madrid Bend and Columbus, a great swamp, which for a part of its extent is a sheet of water called Reelfoot Lake, extends along the left bank of the Mississippi, and discharges its waters into the Mississippi forty miles below Tiptonville, leaving between it and the river the peninsula which lies immediately below Island No. Ten, and opposite New Madrid. Immediately below Tiptonville the swamp for many miles extends entirely to the river. The peninsula is, therefore, substantially an island, having the Mississippi on three sides, and Reelfoot Lake, with its enveloping swamp, on the other. A good road led from the Tennessee shore, opposite Island No. Ten, along the west border of the swamp and the lake to Tiptonville. The only means of supply, therefore, for the forces on Island No. Ten and this peninsula, were by the river. If the river were blockaded at New Madrid, supplies must be landed at Tiptonville and conveyed across the neck of the peninsula by the road. From this peninsula there was no communication with the interior except by a small flatboat which plied across Reelfoot Lake, more than a mile across, by a channel cut through the cypress-trees which cover the lake. Supplies and reinforcements could not, therefore, be brought to any considerable extent by the land side; nor could escape, except by small parties, be made in that direction. A mile below Tiptonville begin the great swamps on both sides of the Mississippi. If batteries could be planted on the lowest dry ground, opposite and below Tiptonville, so as to command the river and effectually intercept navigation, the garrison of Island No. Ten and its supports would be cut off from reinforcements and from escape.

General Polk began the evacuation of Columbus on February 25th. One hundred and forty pieces of artillery were mounted in the works. All these, except two thirty-two-pounders and several carronades, which were spiked and left, were taken to Island No. Ten and the works in connection with it. Brigadier-General McCown with his division went down the river to Island No. Ten, on February 27th, and General Stewart, with a brigade, followed to New Madrid on March 1st. The rest of the infantry marched under General Cheatham, by land, March 1st to Union City. Next day General Polk, having sent off the bulk of the great stores accumulated at this place, destroyed the remainder and moved away with his staff and the cavalry. The force that went from Columbus to Island No. Ten included General Trudeau's command of ten companies of heavy artillery and the Southern Guards who acted as heavy artillery. The light batteries were brigaded with the infantry.

Some progress had been made in throwing up batteries on the island and at the bend. Sappers and miners were at once set to work, aided by the companies of heavy artillery and details from the infantry. By March 12th, four batteries, scarcely above the water-level, were completed on the island and armed with twenty-three guns, and five batteries on the

main-land, armed with twenty-four guns. Battery No. 1, on
the main-land, called the Redan, armed with six guns, was
three thousand yards in an air-line above the point of the
island. A line of infantry intrenchments, *en crémaillère*, extended from the Redan to the water of a bayou which connects
with Reelfoot Lake. A floating battery, anchored near the
lower end of the island, added ten guns to its defence.
Later, a fifth battery was erected on the island, and the number of guns in battery on the island and on the mainland, at
the bend, was increased to fifty-four, exclusive of the floating
battery. On the Missouri shore a bastioned redoubt, called
Fort Thompson, with fourteen guns, stood below the town,
and an earthwork with seven guns, called Fort Bankhead, just
above the town. Infantry intrenchments extended these forts,
and a field-battery of six pieces was added to the armament of
the upper fort. Commodore Hollins, of the Confederate navy,
aided the land-forces with eight gunboats. General McCown,
making an inspecting visit to the position on February 25th,
found there Colonel Gantt, of Arkansas, with the Eleventh
and Twelfth Arkansas, and two artillery companies, acting as
garrison to Fort Thompson, and at once, before returning to
Columbus, ordered Colonel L. M. Walker, with two regiments from Fort Pillow, to guard the defences just above
New Madrid.

General Pope having landed at Commerce with 140 men,
regiments and batteries rapidly arrived from Cairo, St. Louis,
and Cincinnati. With the assistance of able and experienced
officers, Generals Schuyler Hamilton, Stanley, Palmer, and
Granger, the troops were brigaded, divisions formed, and the
command organized. Colonel Plummer being promoted to
brigadier-general after the arrival before New Madrid, the
organization was modified. As finally organized, it comprised
five small infantry divisions. First, commanded by General

D. S. Stanley, comprising First Brigade, Colonel John Groes-beck, Twenty-seventh and Thirty-ninth Ohio; and Second Brigade, Colonel J. L. K. Smith, Forty-third and Sixty-third Ohio. Second Division, General Schuyler Hamilton, comprising First Brigade, Colonel W. H. Worthington, Fifth Iowa and Fifty-ninth Indiana ; and Second Brigade, Colonel N. Perczell, Twenty-sixth Missouri Infantry and Sands' Eleventh Ohio Battery. Third Division, General J. N. Palmer, comprising First Brigade, Colonel J. R. Slack, Thirty-fourth and Forty-seventh Indiana; and Second Brigade, Colonel G. N. Fitch, Forty-third and Forty-sixth Indiana Infantry, Seventh Illinois Cavalry, and Company G, First Missouri Light Artillery. Fourth Division, comprising First Brigade, Colonel J. D. Morgan, Tenth and Sixteenth Illinois ; and Second Brigade, Colonel G. W. Cumming, Twenty-sixth and Fifty-first Illinois, First Illinois Cavalry, and a battalion of Yate's sharpshooters. Fifth Division, General J. B. Plummer, comprising First Brigade, Colonel John Bryner, Forty-seventh Illinois and Eighth Wisconsin ; and Second Brigade, Colonel J. M. Loomis, Twenty-second Illinois, Eleventh Missouri Infantry, and Company M, First Missouri Light Artillery. Besides these was a cavalry division, commanded by General Gordon Granger, comprising the Second and Third Michigan Cavalry; also an artillery division, commanded by Major W. L. Lothrop, comprising the following batteries : Second Iowa, Third Michigan, Company F, Second United States Artillery, Houghtaling's Ottawa Light Artillery, Fifth, Sixth, and Seventh Batteries of the First Wisconsin Artillery, and De Golyer's battery, afterward Company H, of the First Michigan Artillery. In addition to these was a command under Colonel J. W. Bissel, called the Engineer's Regiment of the West, comprising the Fifteenth Wisconsin and Twenty-second Missouri Infantry, the Second Iowa Cavalry, a com-

pany of the Fourth United States Cavalry, a company of the
First United States Infantry, and battalion of the Second Illinois Cavalry. The army commander, the division commanders, and other officers, nearly a dozen in all, were gradu-
ates of West Point. The men of this army had, therefore,
better opportunity than most others to learn quickly something of the business of military life, and acquire habits of
military discipline.

The road from Commerce to New Madrid was, for the most
part, a dilapidated corduroy, tumbling about a broken
causeway through a swamp. M. Jeff. Thompson, "Brigadier-General of the Missouri State Guard," designed to
hold a "very important session of the Missouri Legislature,"
at New Madrid, on March 3d—a session which was to last,
however, but one day. When General Pope moved out from
Commerce, on February 28th, Schuyler Hamilton in front,
Thompson undertook to oppose the advance with a detachment of his irregular command and three light pieces of
rifled artillery. The Seventh Illinois Cavalry charged, captured the three guns, took two officers and several enlisted
men prisoners, and chased Thompson and the rest of his
band sixteen miles, almost to the outskirts of New Madrid.
Dragging through the mud by short marches, Hamilton's
division reached New Madrid on the morning of March 3d.
Deploying, with the Twenty-seventh and Thirty-ninth Ohio
in front as skirmishers, Hamilton marched upon the town,
pushed the enemy's pickets back into the intrenchments,
developed the line of intrenchment, drew the fire of its
armament—twenty-four, thirty-two, and sixty-four pounders
and field-pieces. The gunboats of Commodore Hollins'
fleet took part in the engagement. The water in the river
was so high that it lifted the guns on the boats above the
banks. The reconnoissance developed the fact that the in-

trenchments could be carried by assault, but could not be held so long as the gunboats could lay the muzzles of their heavy guns upon the river-bank and sweep the whole interior.

The reconnoissance made by General Hamilton showed the necessity of having siege-guns. The troops were put into camp about two miles back from the river; urgent request was sent to Cairo for heavy artillery, and parties were pushed forward every day to harass the garrison and keep them occupied. Colonel Plummer (soon after brigadier-general and commanding a division of his own) was detached from Hamilton's division and sent with the Eleventh Missouri, Twenty-sixth and Forty-seventh Illinois Infantry, four guns of the First Missouri Light Artillery, and one company of engineer troops, together with two companies of cavalry, to act as outpost toward the interior—to Point Pleasant. The object was to attempt by field-pieces to stop the passage of transport steamboats up and down the river. Colonel Plummer, leaving camp at noon, March 5th, proceeding by a circuitous road to avoid passing along the river-bank, halted for the night in bivouac, without fires, within three or four miles of the town. A gunboat prevented his cavalry and artillery from occupying the town next day, but was driven away by the fire of the infantry. The infantry and engineers prosecuted the work of digging rifle-pits, and in the night places were sunk for the field-pieces by excavating near the edge of the bank. By morning of March 7th the four guns were in position, planted apart, with lines of rifle-pits connecting them. When discovered, the gunboats immediately began a furious assault. Plummer's artillery wasted no ammunition in useless fire upon the iron-plated boats, and his guns were so shielded by their position in sunken batteries, back from the edge of the bank, that the

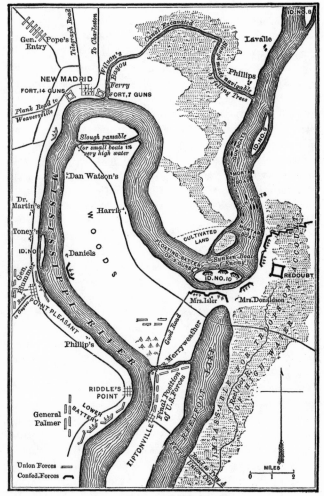

New Madrid and Island Number Ten.

II.—4

fire of the gunboats passed harmless overhead. The deliberate fire of sharpshooters from the rifle-pits, however,
searching every opened porthole, pilot-house, and every exposed point, was so annoying that the fleet withdrew. Every
day the gunboats opened upon the position, either in stationary attack or while passing up and down the river. But, to
avoid the harassing fire from the rifle-pits, they kept, after
the first few attacks, near the opposite shore of the river.
The steamboats used as transports did not venture to pass
up or down the river in face of Plummer's batteries, and
the enemy was restricted to the landing at Tiptonville and
boats below for all communication.

On the 6th, General Pope telegraphed that Colonel Plummer had not yet been able to effect his lodgement at Point
Pleasant, but that the sharpshooters were trying to drive
the artillerymen of the gunboats from their pieces. Next
day, the 7th, General Halleck telegraphed to Pope : "After
securing the roads so as to prevent the enemy's advance
north, you will withdraw your remaining forces to Sikeston,
and thence to Bird's Point or Commerce for embarkation.
They will proceed up the Tennessee to reinforce General C.
F. Smith. Good luck." On the same day, the 7th, General
Pope reported by telegraph Plummer's success in establish-
ing himself, and nothing more was heard about abandoning
the expedition.

General Pope had asked for rifled thirty-twos. General
Cullum, Halleck's chief of staff, who was stationed at Cairo
and had immediate charge and supervision of sending reinforcements and supplies to the armies in Halleck's department, not finding rifled thirty-twos, obtained three twenty-
four-pounders and one eight-inch howitzer. Colonel Bissell,
of the engineer regiment, who was in Cairo waiting for them,
received these four pieces on March 11th. They were

shipped across the river to Bird's Point, and sent by rail to
Sikeston. At Sikeston a detachment from the company of
regular artillery, with horses, as well as the regiment of engineers, were waiting. The pieces were quickly unshipped
and mounted on carriages. The engineers had such success
in repairing the road, and the artillery in conducting the
pieces, that all arrived in good order about sunset of the
12th.

Major Lathrop, commanding the artillery, had, on the
11th, reconnoitered the ground and selected a position about
eight hundred yards in front of Fort Thompson, for batteries to contain the siege-guns. On Colonel Bissell's arrival,
he went again to the front and pointed out the position selected. About dusk, two companies of the Thirty-ninth
Ohio, deployed as skirmishers, drove back the enemy's pickets toward the works. At nine o'clock P.M., Colonel Bissell
and Major Lathrop arrived on the ground with Colonel
Morgan, who had with him the Tenth and six companies of
the Sixteenth Illinois. The Tenth Illinois, advancing in
open order, pushed the enemy's pickets still farther back
and close to their works. The six companies of the Sixteenth followed with picks and spades. Two companies of
the Tenth, deployed as skirmishers, were pushed forward,
covering the front and flanks of the party, with orders not
to fire even if fired upon. The remaining eight companies
of the Tenth Illinois joined the Sixteenth as a working party.
The lines of two batteries for two guns each, and lines of
infantry intrenchments, had now been traced. The fourteen
companies worked with such zeal that the works were completed by three o'clock A. M. Captain Mower, of the First
United States Infantry, who, with Companies A and H of his
regiment, had been put in command of the siege-artillery, put
the four pieces in position; Colonel Morgan, recalling his

pickets, posted his command in the trenches. General Stanley moved out with his division in support, and, at daylight, Mower opened fire upon Fort Thompson.

The force in Forts Thompson and Bankhead numbered about three thousand effectives, according to General A. P. Stewart, who had general command of both; thirty-five hundred, according to General Gantt, who commanded at Fort Thompson, and had been promoted after being assigned to the command. The fire from Captain Mower's guns was the first notice General Gantt or his men had of the erection of the batteries. Fort Thompson replied with all its guns. Fort Bankhead joined with its heavy ordnance and field-battery. Commodore Hollins brought his fleet close in shore and aided the bombardment. Captain Mower, by direction of General Pope, paid little heed to the forts, but directed most of his fire to the boats. The forts on either side were little injured. One twenty-four pounder in Mower's battery, and one thirty-two in Fort Thompson, were disabled. The gunboats were struck, but not seriously injured.

In the evening, General McCown visited Commodore Hollins on his flag-ship, and, after a conference, sent for General Stewart. Commodore Hollins stated that he had been positively assured that heavy artillery could not be brought over the wet and swampy country, and he was not prepared to encounter it. General McCown said it was evident to him that Pope intended, by regular approaches, to cut off Fort Thompson. He told A. P. Stewart that reinforcements could not be expected within ten days. Stewart said he could not hold out three days. All agreed, then, that the forts must be evacuated, and immediately.

About ten o'clock P.M. a gunboat and two transports reported to Colonel Walker at Fort Bankhead, and General Stewart proceeded with two gunboats to Fort Thompson.

According to Colonel Walker's report, the evacuation and embarkation at his post was orderly, though impeded by a heavy rain-storm, and restricted by the very insufficient transportation afforded by the boats. He was unable to carry off any of the heavy guns, but succeeded in shipping the guns of Bankhead's field-battery, leaving their limbers and caissons behind. General Gantt's report represents a like state of affairs at Fort Thompson. But, according to General Stewart's report, his directions were imperfectly carried out. One twenty-four pounder was pulled off its platform into the swamp in its rear, where it sank so deep in the mud that it was impossible to move it. No attempt was made to remove more. The storm began at eleven o'clock. "The rain was unusually violent, and the night became so dark that it was difficult to see, except by the flashes of lightning. The men became sullen and indifferent—indisposed to work. I spent some time in collecting together such of them as were idle and urged them to carry off the boxes of ammunition from the magazine, and pass them aboard the boat. At length I learned from Captain Stewart that all the guns had been spiked, that rat-tail files had been sent up for the purpose from one of the gunboats, with orders to spike the guns. I replied that no such orders had been given by me, that the spiking of the guns should have been the last thing done." "Soon after this an artillery officer informed me that Gantt's regiment was going aboard the boats, that Captain Carter was hurrying them, telling them he intended to save his boats, and would leave them to shift for themselves if the enemy fired." "I directed the artillery officers, before the boats left, to make an effort to get their tents on board. They subsequently reported that they could not get many of the men together in the darkness and rain, nor induce the few whom they did collect to do anything at it." General

Stewart ordered the pickets who had been sent out to cover the movement to be recalled, and the tents and quarters to be searched. Thirteen men, however, were left. One of the gunboats took in tow a wharf-boat at the landing, which was used as a hospital and contained several hundred sick. Between three and four o'clock in the morning the boats pulled out and left.

Morgan's brigade, after constructing the works in the night of the 12th, remained in the trenches till relieved early in the morning of the 14th. At two o'clock A.M. of the 14th, General Hamilton advanced with his division to relieve General Stanley in support, and with Slack's brigade of Palmer's division to relieve Morgan's brigade in the trenches. "The darkness was palpable, the rain poured down in torrents, the men were obliged to wade through pools knee-deep. Silence having been strictly enjoined, the division, hoping to have the honor of leading in the assault on the enemy's works, moved steadily forward with cheerful alacrity; those assigned to that duty taking post in the rifle-pits half full of water, without a murmur." A heavy fog obscured the dawn. About six o'clock two deserters reported that the fort had been hastily abandoned in the night, after a portion of the guns had been spiked. Captain Mower and Lieutenant Fletcher, commanding the two companies in charge of the siege-guns, were dispatched into the fort to hoist the American flag. Two field-batteries, besides the heavy artillery, great quantities of ammunition for small arms as well as for the artillery, tents, stores of all sorts, the wagons, horses, and mules of the troops at Fort Thompson, were found. The wagons and animals at Fort Bankhead had been sent across the river a few days before. General Beauregard, whose command included these defences, ordered an inquiry into the facts of the evacuation of New Madrid. The inspecting officer reported substantially in accordance with the report of General A. P. Stewart.

Immediately the evacuation was confirmed, Hamilton's division was moved into the works and their guns were turned toward the river. Without delay, batteries were at night sunk at points along the river just back of the river-bank, and the captured siege-guns, hauled laboriously by hand down the the strip of more solid ground-between the river and swamp, were placed in position in them. The lowest battery was below Point Pleasant, and opposite and a little below Tiptonville. This extended General Pope's line seventeen miles along the river. The lowest battery commanded the lowest solid ground on the Tennessee shore—all below was swamp. This battery, if maintained, cut off the enemy alike from retreat, and from reinforcements and supplies. When the morning of the 15th disclosed the muzzles of the heavy guns peering over the river-bank as over a parapet, five gunboats moved up within three hundred yards, and with furious cannonade strove to destroy them. In an hour and a half one gunboat was sunk, others damaged, gunners on them shot from the rifle-pits on shore, and the fleet retired.

On March 15th, Commodore Foote moved with his fleet of gunboats and mortar-boats to the neighborhood of Island No. 10, and next day engaged the batteries on the island and the main-land, at long range, to ascertain their position and armament. Next day five gunboats and four mortar-boats moved down to within two thousand yards of the upper battery or redan, and opened fire. The batteries on main-land and island replied. One hundred pieces of heavy ordnance rent the quivering air with their thunder. The rampart of the redan had been constructed twenty-four feet thick, but the high water beating against it had washed it, and, by percolation, softened it. The heavy shot from the gunboats

passed though it. Thirteen-inch shells exploding in the
ground made caverns in the soil. Water stood on the ground
within, and the artillerists waded in mud and water. The
conflict lasted till evening. The staff of the signal-flag used
in the redan was shattered by a shot; but the officer, Lieutenant Jones, picking up the flag, and using his arm as a
staff, continued signalling. The rampart of the redan was
torn and ridged, and one sixty-four gun was dismounted and
another injured, an officer killed, and seven enlisted men
wounded. On the island a one hundred and twenty-eight
pound gun burst. In the fleet a gun burst on the Pittsburg,
killing and wounding fourteen men.

The fleet and batteries exchanged fire with greater or less
severity every day. On the 21st, another large gun, called
the Belmont, burst on the island. In the course of these
engagements the redan was finally knocked to pieces and
ceased to reply; and, on April 1st, an expedition from the
fleet landed, drove off a detachment of the First Alabama
which was guarding it, and spiked its guns. The work of
erecting new batteries and mounting guns, as well as repairing damages, was continued as long as the island was occupied.

On the night of March 17th, General McCown left for
Fort Pillow with the Eleventh, Twelfth, and Colonel Ken-
nedy's Louisiana, Fourth, Fifth, and Thirty-first Tennessee,
Bankhead's and six guns of Captain R. C. Stewart's batteries, and Neely's and Haywood's cavalry, leaving at Madrid Bend the First Alabama, Eleventh and Twelfth Arkansas,
and Terry's Arkansas Battalion, three Tennessee regiments,
commanded respectively by Colonels Brown, Clark, and
Henderson, Colonel Baker's regiment of twelve companies
called the Tennessee, Alabama, and Mississippi regiment, five
guns of Captain Stewart's field-battery, and Captain Hud-

son's and Captain Wheeler's cavalry. Besides these were
the companies of heavy artillery, and what other troops, on
the island and below, the reports do not show. Most, if not
all of the troops taken to Fort Pillow by General McCown,
proceeded to Corinth and joined the force which General A.
S. Johnston was gathering there. General McCown on his
return arrived below Tiptonville on March 20th, and established his headquarters at Madrid Bend next day.

General Pope had now established his army and batteries
on the right bank of the river, so as to prevent the escape of
the enemy until the river should fall. To capture them he
must cross the river. General Halleck telegraphed to him
on March 16th to construct a road, if possible, through the
swamp above the bayou, which comes into the river just
above New Madrid, to a point on the Missouri shore opposite
Island No. Ten, and transfer thither enough of his force to
erect batteries and aid the fleet in the bombardment of the
island. Pope despatched Colonel Bissell to examine the
country with this view, directing him at the same time, if he
found it impracticable to build the road, to ascertain if it
were possible to dig a canal across the peninsula, from some
point above the island to New Madrid. The idea of the
canal was suggested to General Pope by General Schuyler
Hamilton, an officer whose gentle refinement veiled his absolute resolution and endurance till they were called into
practice by danger and privation.

Colonel Bissell found no place where a road could be constructed ; but, by following up the bayou (called John's Bayou
in the Confederate reports, called Wilson's Bayou on the
map made by the United States engineers) which comes
into the river immediately above New Madrid, he traced it
into the swamp and found that, in connection with depressions and sloughs, a continuous, though tortuous water-way

6

could be gained at that high stage of water, from a point in
the river between Islands Eight and Nine and the river at
New Madrid. The length of this channel was twelve miles.
Part of it had to be excavated to get sufficient depth; for
six miles it passed through a thick forest of large trees.

General Pope immediately sent to Cairo for four light-
draught steamers, and tools, implements, and supplies needed
to cut a navigable way. Colonel Bissell was at once ordered
to set his entire command at work, and to call upon the land
force on the fleet for aid if needed. For six miles Bissell
had to cut through the forest a channel fifty feet wide and
four and a half feet deep. Sawing through the trunks of
large trees four and a half feet under the surface of the cold
water was a work of extreme toil and great exposure. The
trees when felled had to be disentangled, cut up, and thrust
among the standing trees. Overhanging boughs of trees,
growing outside the channel, had to be lopped off. Shallow
places were excavated. The whole had to be done from the
decks of the little working-boats, or by men standing in the
water. The men were urged to incessant labor; yet they
toiled with such ardor that urging was not needed. General
Halleck telegraphed to Pope, Friday, March 21st, that he
would not hamper him with any minute instructions, but
would leave him to accomplish the object according to his
own judgment, and added: " Buell will be with Grant and
Smith by Monday." In nineteen days, April 4th, the way
was open and clear; and on the 5th, steamers and barges
were brought through near to the lower mouth, but not near
enough to be in view from the river.

The Confederate officers on the island were aware of the
attempt to secure this cut-off across the peninsula. Captain
Gray, engineer, in a report or memorandum, dated March
29th, spoke of " the canal being cut by the enemy," and

of heavy guns planted to be used against any boat that might issue from the bayou, as well as batteries erected along the shore, from about a mile and a half below New Madrid down to Tiptonville. But General McCown, when turning over the command to General W. W. Mackall, who relieved him on March 31st, said to him that the National troops were endeavoring to cut a canal across the peninsula, but they would fail, and that Mackall would find the position safe until the river fell, but no longer.

The task which General Pope had proposed to himself—to cross a wide, deep, rapid river, in the face of an enemy holding the farther shore in force, was sufficiently arduous at first. Now that Captain Gray's industry had lined the river-shore with batteries armed with twenty-four, thirty-two, and sixty-four pound guns, and eight-inch howitzers and columbiads, sufficient to blow out of the water any unarmed steamer that should venture to cross, the task was impracticable with his present resources. He applied to Commodore Foote, and urgently repeated the application, for two gunboats, or even one, to be sent down the river some dark night to engage these batteries below New Madrid. But the Commodore was not willing to risk his boats in a voyage along the front of miles of batteries, and declined. On March 28th Halleck telegraphed: "I have telegraphed to Commodore Foote to give you all the aid in his power. You have a difficult problem to solve. I will not embarrass you with instructions. I leave you to act as your judgment may deem best."

Pope set to work to make floating-batteries, to be manned by his troops. Each battery consisted of three heavy barges, lashed together and bolted with iron. The middle barge was bulkheaded all around, so as to have four feet of thickness of solid timber at both the ends and the sides. Three heavy guns were mounted on it and protected by traverses

of sand-bags. It also carried eighty sharpshooters. The
barges outside of it had a first layer, in the bottom, of empty
water-tight barrels, securely lashed, then layers of dry cot-
ton-wood rails and cotton-bales packed close. These were
floored over at the top to keep everything in place, so that
a shot penetrating the outer barges would have to pass
through twenty feet of rails and cotton before reaching the
middle one, which carried the men and guns. The outer
barges, thus bulkheaded with water-tight barrels and buoy-
ant cotton-bales, could not sink. These barges, when all
was ready, were to be towed by steamers to a point directly
opposite New Madrid. This could be done safely, as the
shore at the point and for a mile and a half below was
swamp, and the nearest battery was necessarily below the
swamp. When near the opposite shore the floating-batteries
were to be cut loose from the steamers and allowed to float
down-stream to the point selected for the landing of the
troops. As soon as they arrived within short range they
were to drop anchor and open fire.

Meanwhile Commander Henry Walke had volunteered to
take his boat, the Carondelet; and, on March 30th, Flag-
officer Foote gave him permission to make the attempt on
the first dark night. The morning of April 4th was a busy
time on the Carondelet. The deck was covered with heavy
planks, surplus chains were coiled over the most vulnerable
parts of the boat, an eleven-inch hawser was wound around
the pilot-house as high as the windows ; barriers of cord-
wood were built about the boilers. After sunset, the at-
mosphere became hazy and the sky overcast. Guns were
run back, ports closed, and the sailors armed to resist
boarders. Directions were given to sink the boat if it became liable to fall into the enemy's hands. At dusk, twenty
sharpshooters from the Forty-second Illinois came aboard to

be ready to aid the crew in resisting boarders. After dark, a coal-barge laden with baled hay was fastened to the port side of the boat.

At ten o'clock the moon had gone down and a storm was gathering. The Carondelet cast loose and steamed slowly down the river. The machinery was adjusted so as to permit the steam to escape through the wheel-house, and avoid the noise of puffing through the pipes. The boat glided noiseless and invisible through the darkness. Scarcely had it advanced half a mile when the soot in the chimneys caught fire, a blaze shot up five feet above the smoke-stack. The flue-caps were opened, the blaze subsided, and all was yet silent along the shore. The soot in the smoke-stacks not being moistened by the steam, which was now escaping through the wheel-house, became very inflammable. Just as the Carondelet was passing by the upper battery—the redan—the treacherous flame again leaped from the chimneys, revealing and proclaiming the mission of the boat. Sentries on the parapets on shore fired, guards turned out, rockets darted skyward ; the heavy guns opened fire ; and the brooding storm broke forth, the lightning and thunder above drowning the flashes and war below. The lightning revealed the position of the gunboat, but it also disclosed the outline of the shore, enabling the pilots to steer with certainty. The boat was pushed near to the Tennessee shore and to the island, and put to its greatest speed. Impeded by the barge in tow, its greatest speed was slow progress, and for half an hour the gunners in the batteries watched the black night to see the hurrying Carondelet shot for an instant out of the darkness at every lightning flash. Beyond the batteries lay the floating battery, carrying nine guns, which had been driven from its moorings the day before by the heavy fire of the fleet. A light on the floating battery marked its position.

A few shots left it, but it evinced no eagerness to join in conflict. The Carondelet, unharmed, untouched, fired the agreed signal, and fleet and army knew at midnight the passage was a success.

On the morning of the sixth, Commander Walke, taking on board General Granger, Colonel Smith, of the Forty-third Ohio, and Captain L. H. Marshall, of General Pope's staff, steamed down the river under a heavy fire from the batteries that lined the Tennessee shore, ascertained the position of the batteries, and, on the return silenced the batteries opposite Point Pleasant. Captain Marshall landed with a party and spiked the guns. In the night of the 6th, Commodore Foote, in compliance with General Pope's earnest request, sent the gunboat Pittsburg down to New Madrid, where it arrived, like the Carondelet, untouched.

At the break of day of the 7th, in a heavy rain, Captain Williams, of the First United States Infantry, opened with his thirty-two pounders upon the batteries opposite him at Watson's Landing, where General Pope proposed to land his troops. Commander Walke, with the two gunboats, silenced the batteries along the shore. Three sixty-four pound guns, standing half a mile apart, were spiked. A battery of two sixty-four pound howitzers and one sixty-four pound gun maintained a contest till two of the pieces were dismounted and the other disabled. The four steamers came out of the bayou and took on board Paine's division. At noon, Commander Walke signalled that all the batteries to Watson's Landing were silenced and the way was clear. A spy in the employment of General Pope, who had been taken from the Tennessee shore by Commander Walke and forwarded by him to General Pope, brought the news that the forces about Madrid Bend were in full retreat to Tiptonville. Paine's division, sailing by just at that time, was signalled to stop, and the news was communicated, with orders to land and push in pursuit to Tiptonville with all dispatch. Colonel Morgan's brigade moved in advance, followed by Colonel Cumming's brigade and Houghtaling's battery. Abandoned camps and artillery were passed ; prisoners were gathered up. A detachment of cavalry fled as the column came in sight. About nine miles from the landing, General Mackall was found well posted, with infantry, artillery, and cavalry. The leading regiment deployed in line, and General Mackall retired. Twice again he halted in line as if to make a stand, and retreated as the National troops approached. At night Morgan's brigade halted at Tiptonville, and found shelter from the rain in an abandoned camp. The pickets of the brigade gathered in 359 prisoners in the night. Cumming's brigade, being ordered to explore the road coming from the north into the one over which they were moving, came upon the river shore opposite the island, and learned from a few prisoners taken there that but few troops were left on the island. Finding no boats or other means of getting over to the island, Cumming returned to the south, and marched till he came near the camp-fires of the enemy, and then went into bivouac and advised General Paine of his position. General Mackall found himself hemmed in to the south and east by swamp, and to the north and west by Paine's division. Two hours after midnight his adjutant-general took to General Paine General Mackall's unconditional surrender.

Stanley's division followed Paine's, and was followed by Hamilton's. These were overtaken by night and went into bivouac about half way between the crossing and Tiptonville, and learned of the surrender next morning while on the way to join Paine. Colonel Elliott, of the Second Iowa Cavalry, sent with two of his companies by General Pope at dawn of the 8th from Watson's up the river-bank, captured two hundred prisoners, deck-hands and laborers as well as soldiers, the wharf-boat and steamers, great quantities of ordnance and other stores, and standing camps. Turning these over to Colonel Buford, who commanded the land forces on the fleet, and who came over to shore from the island on a steamer, he joined the forces at Tiptonville.

Lieutenant-Colonel Cook, commanding the Twelfth Arkansas, was appointed commandant of the island by General Mackall on the morning of the 7th. Lieutenant-Colonel Cook received, simultaneously with the order, information of Mackall's retreat, and General Pope's landing and pursuit. In the evening he abandoned the island with his regiment, and turned over the command of the island to Captain Humes, of the artillery. Before daylight of the 8th, Commodore Foote was visited by two officers from the island, who tendered a surrender of it and all on it. A gunboat was sent to ascertain the state of affairs. Having learned three hours later of the crossing of the river by Pope, the flight of General Mackall, and the evacuation of the shore-batteries, he sent Colonel Buford, with a force of two gunboats, to receive possession of the island. Seventeen officers and three hundred and sixty-eight privates surrendered to him, besides the two hundred sick and employees turned over to him by Colonel Elliott. Lieutenant-Colonel Cook found his way through the swamp, on the night of the 7th, to the ferry across Reelfoot Lake. In the course of the night he was joined by about four hundred fugitives, mostly belonging to his own regiment, many of them just from the hospital. Hungry, and cold, and drenched with rain, they stood in the water waiting till they could be carried over the lake, through the cypress trees, in two small flatboats and on some extemporized rafts. It was noon of the 9th before the forlorn band were all over, and, without knapsacks or blankets, many without arms, began their weary march for Memphis.

All the troops but Cumming's brigade returned to their camps on the Missouri shore on the 8th. Colonel Cumming, having charge of the prisoners, returned on the evening of the 9th. General Pope, in his final detailed report giving the result of all the operations, states: "Three generals, two hundred and seventy-three field and company officers, six thousand seven hundred privates, one hundred and twenty-three pieces of heavy artillery, thirty-five pieces of field artillery, all of the very best character and of the latest patterns, seven thousand stand of small arms, tents for twelve thousand men, several wharf-boat loads of provisions, an immense quantity of ammunition of all kinds, many hundred horses and mules, with wagons and harness, etc., are among the spoils." The capture embraced, besides, six steamboats—two of them sunk—the gunboat Grampus, carrying two guns, sunk; and the floating battery, carrying nine guns, which the crew had ineffectually attempted to scuttle before abandoning it. Two of the generals captured were brigadier-generals, Mackall and Gantt; the third was perhaps L. M. Walker. When Major-General McCown was relieved on March 31st by Mackall, McCown and Brigadier-General Trudeau left. Brigadier-General A. P. Stewart had left previously and reported for duty at Corinth. Colonels Walker and Gantt were promoted brigadier-generals after the siege began. General Walker appears, from his report of April 9th, dated St. Francis County, Arkansas, to have left on account of ill-health some time before the surrender. The prisoners embraced, including those on the island surrendered to the navy, seven regiments and one battalion of infantry, one of the regiments having twelve companies—eleven companies of heavy and one of light artillery, two companies of cavalry, the officers and crews of the floating battery and the steamboats, and laborers and employees.

The Mississippi was now open to Fort Pillow. General Halleck telegraphed to General Pope : "I congratulate you and your command on your splendid achievement. It exceeds in boldness and brilliancy all other operations of the war. It will be memorable in military history, and will be admired by future generations." On April 12th, General Pope and his entire command embarked on transports and steamed down the river, in company with the gunboat fleet. The force arrived in front of Fort Pillow on the 14th. In a few days, before reconnoitring was completed, Pope was ordered to report with his whole command, except two regiments to be left with the gunboats, to General Halleck at Pittsburg Landing.

CHAPTER V.

THE GATHERING OF THE FORCES.

AFTER the surrender of Fort Donelson, the force confronting Halleck was the command of General Beauregard, stationed at Columbus, Island Number Ten, at Forts Pillow and Randolph, at Memphis, and at convenient points on the railroads in Mississippi. The next objective point that presented itself was Memphis, and, as preliminary, the fortified points on the river above it. But Memphis had large railway connections. The direct road to Nashville was cut at its crossing over the Tennessee River, but at Humboldt it intersected the Mobile and Ohio, which joined Columbus with Mobile. The Memphis and Charleston, running nearly due east to Chattanooga, also intersected the Mobile and Ohio at Corinth. The Mississippi and Tennessee, in connection with the New Orleans, Jackson and Great Northern, gave a route nearly due south to New Orleans, and this intersected at Jackson, Mississippi, another road running east, and which needed only a connecting link between Selma and Montgomery, Alabama, to make it also a through route to the Atlantic States. To destroy the junction at Humboldt would cut off railway connection with Columbus. To destroy the junction at Corinth would cut off connection with the east. A little eastwardly of Corinth, near Eastport, was a considerable railroad bridge over Bear Creek. General Halleck's first step, therefore, was to break these railway connections, and as General A. S.

Johnston was falling back southwardly, it became doubly important to sever these connections for the purpose of preventing a conjunction of the forces under Johnston and Beauregard. Lieutenant-Commander Phelps had gone up to Florence, at the foot of Muscle Shoals, immediately after the surrender of Fort Henry, without difficulty. An expedition up the Tennessee, to send out strong, light parties, suggested itself as the natural means of accomplishing the first step. General Halleck proposed to accomplish this by his lieutenants before taking the field in person.

Halleck was sedate, deliberate, cautious. He had written a book on strategy and logistics, and his attention appeared sometimes to be distracted from the actual conditions under which the present military operations were to be conducted by his retrospective reference to the rules which he had announced. Grant, under his extremely quiet demeanor, was full of restless activity. His purpose seemed to be to strike and overcome the enemy without waiting; to use whatever seemed the best means at hand; ready at all times to change for better means if they could be found; but never to cease striking. Halleck was worried by being jogged to new enterprises, but heartily supported them when once begun. C. F. Smith had a brusque manner, but a warm heart. He was direct and honest as a child. He seemed impetuous, but his outburst was a rush of controlled power. He was a thorough soldier, an enthusiast in his profession, the soul of honor, the type of discipline. His commanding officer was to him embodied law; it would have been impossible for him to conceive that his duty and subordination could in any way be affected by the fact that his pupil in the Military Academy had become his commander.

General Grant, being commander of the Military District of Western Tennessee, with limits undefined, sent General

C. F. Smith from Fort Donelson, fifty miles up the river to Clarksville, to take possession of the place and the railway bridge over the river there. General Grant wrote to General Cullum, advising him of this movement and proposing the capture of Nashville, but adding he was ready for any move the General Commanding might direct. On the 24th he wrote to General Cullum, General Halleck's chief of staff, that he had sent four regiments to Clarksville, and would send no more till he heard from General Halleck. Next day he wrote that the head of Buell's column had reached Nashville, and he would go there on the receipt of the next mail, unless it should contain some orders preventing him. He went to Nashville on the 27th, and returned to Fort Donelson next day. In his absence there was, among some of the troops about Fort Donelson, fresh from civil life and restive under the inactivity and restraint of a winter camp, some disorder and insubordination. There was, moreover, some marauding in which officers participated. General Grant, on his return, published orders repressing such practices, arrested the guilty parties and sent the arrested officers to St. Louis to report to General Halleck.

On March 1st General Halleck sent to General Grant, from St. Louis, an order directing the course of immediate operations : " Transports will be sent to you as soon as possible to move your column up the Tennessee River. The main object of this expedition will be to destroy the railroad bridge over Bear Creek, near Eastport, Miss., and also the connections at Corinth, Jackson, and Humboldt. It is thought best that these objects should be attempted in the order named. Strong detachments of cavalry and light artillery, supported by infantry, may, by rapid movements, reach these points from the river without very serious opposition. Avoid any general engagement with strong forces.

It will be better to retreat than to risk a general battle. This should be strongly impressed upon the officers sent with the expedition from the river. General C. F. Smith, or some very discreet officer, should be selected for such commands. Having accomplished these objects, or such of them as may be practicable, you will return to Danville and move on Paris. . . . Competent officers should be left to command the garrisons of Forts Henry and Donelson in your absence. . . ." General Grant received the order on March 2d, and repaired at once to Fort Henry. On the 4th the forces at Fort Donelson marched across to the Tennessee, where they were speedily joined by Sherman's division and other reinforcements coming by boat up the river.

On March 2d General Halleck, having received an anonymous letter reflecting on General Grant, telegraphed to General McClellan, the General-in-Chief, at Washington : " I have had no communication with General Grant for more than a week. He left his command without my authority, and went to Nashville. His army seems to be as much demoralized by the victory of Fort Donelson as was that of the Potomac by the defeat of Bull Run. It is hard to censure a successful general immediately after a victory, but I think he richly deserves it. I can get no reports, no returns, no information of any kind from him. Satisfied with his victory, he sits down and enjoys it without any regard to the future. I am worn out and tired by this neglect and inefficiency. C. F. Smith is almost the only officer equal to the emergency." Next day McClellan answered by telegraph : " The future success of our cause demands that proceedings such as General Grant's should at once be checked. Generals must observe discipline as well as private soldiers. Do not hesitate to arrest him at once if the good of the service requires it, and place C. F. Smith in command. You are at

liberty to regard this as a positive order, if it will smooth
your way." On the 4th General Halleck telegraphed to
Grant : " You will place Major-General C. F. Smith in command of expedition, and remain yourself at Fort Henry.
Why do you not obey my orders to report strength and
position of your command ? " Grant replied next day :
" Troops will be sent under command of Major-General
Smith, as directed. I had prepared a different plan, intend-
ing General Smith to command the forces which should go
to Paris and Humboldt, while I would command the expedition upon Eastport, Corinth, and Jackson in person. . . .
I am not aware of ever having disobeyed any order from
your headquarters—certainly never intended such a thing.
I have reported almost daily the condition of my command,
and reported every position occupied. . . ." An inter-
change of telegrams of substantially the same tenor, General Halleck's gradually losing their asperity, lasted a week
longer. On March 10th, the day before the President, by
War Order No. 3, relieved General McClellan from the supreme command of the armies, General L. Thomas, Adjutant-General of the Army, wrote to General-Halleck : " It has
been reported that, soon after the battle of Fort Donelson,
Brigadier-General Grant left his command without leave.
By direction of the President, the Secretary of War directs
you to ascertain and report whether General Grant left his
command at any time without proper authority, and if so,
for how long ; whether he has made to you proper reports
and returns of his forces ; whether he has committed any
acts which were unauthorized or not in accordance with military subordination or propriety, and if so, what ? " On the
13th Halleck telegraphed to Grant, who had asked to be
relieved if his course was not satisfactory, or until he could
be set right : " You cannot be relieved from your command.

There is no good reason for it. I am certain that all which the authorities at Washington ask is, that you enforce discipline and punish the disorderly. . . . Instead of relieving you, I wish you, as soon as your new army is in the field, to assume the immediate command and lead it on to new victories." To this Grant replied next day : " After your letter enclosing copy of an anonymous letter upon which severe censure was based, I felt as though it would be impossible for me to serve longer without a court of inquiry. Your telegram of yesterday, however, places such a different phase upon my position that I will again assume command, and give every effort to the success of our cause. Under the worst circumstances I would do the same." On the 15th General Halleck replied to the Adjutant-General of the Army, fully exonerating General Grant. General C. F. Smith felt keenly the injustice done to Grant, and gladly relinquished command of the expedition when Grant assumed it.

Meanwhile the army with its stores had been gathering on a fleet of boats between Fort Henry and the railroad bridge. To the three divisions of Fort Donelson, First, Second, and Third, commanded by C. F. Smith, McClernand, and Lewis Wallace, were added a fourth, commanded by Brigadier-General S. A. Hurlbut, and a fifth by Brigadier-General W. T. Sherman. While C. F. Smith commanded the expedition, his division was commanded by W. H. L. Wallace, who had been promoted to brigadier-general. The steamer Golden State, with one-half of the Fortieth Illinois, reached Savannah, on the right bank of the river, on March 5th. The Forty-sixth Ohio arrived the next day. Behind these was the fleet of more than eighty steamboats, carrying the five divisions and convoyed by three gunboats, a vast procession extending miles along the winding river, each boat with its pillar of smoke by day, and of fire by night. The fleet began arriving at Savannah on the 11th, and lined both shores of the river. Lewis Wallace's division sent a party to the railroad west of the river, striking it at Purdy, tearing up a portion, but doing no permanent injury, and returned. On the 14th, General Smith sent Sherman's division up the river to strike the railroad near Eastport. Rain fell in torrents, roads melted into mud, and small streams rose with dangerous rapidity. The expedition, arrested by an unfordable torrent, returned just in time to reach the landing by wading through water waist-deep. The boats left in the night of the 15th, and stopped at Pittsburg Landing, on the west bank of the river, about nine miles above Savannah. Hurlbut's division was already on boats at this landing, having been ordered thither by General C. F. Smith on the evening of the 14th.

The first step in the programme laid down in General Halleck's order of March 1st, the destruction of the railroad near Eastport, had failed, and events had now required a material change in the programme. General Buell on March 3d telegraphed to Halleck : "What can I do to aid your operations against Columbus?" Halleck, replying next day that Columbus was evacuated and destroyed, added : "Why not come to the Tennessee and operate with me to cut Johnston's line with Memphis, Randolph, and New Madrid. . . . Estimated strength of enemy at New Madrid, Randolph and Memphis is fifty thousand. It is of vital importance to separate them from Johnston's army. Come over to Savannah or Florence, and we can do it. We can then operate on Decatur or Memphis, or both, as may appear best." Buell rejoined on the 5th : "The thing I think of vital importance is that you seize and hold the bridge at Florence in force." On the 6th Halleck telegraphed : "News

down the Tennessee that Beauregard has twenty thousand
men at Corinth, and is rapidly fortifying it. Smith will
probably not be strong enough to attack it. It is a great
misfortune to lose that point. I shall reinforce Smith as
rapidly as possible. If you can send a division by water
around into the Tennessee, it would require only a small
amount of transportation to do it." To this Buell telegraphed on the 9th, insisting on his suggestions made on the
5th. Halleck dispatched on the 10th : "My forces are moving up the Tennessee River as rapidly as we can obtain transportation. Florence was the point originally designated, but,
on account of the enemy's forces at Corinth and Humboldt,
it is deemed best to land at Savannah and establish a depot.
The transportation will serve as ferries. The selection is left
to C. F. Smith, who commands the advance. . . . You
do not say whether we are to expect any reinforcements from
Nashville." On the same day Buell telegraphed : ". . .
The establishment of your force on this side of the river, as
high up as possible, is evidently judicious. . . . I can
join you almost, if not quite as soon, by water, in better condition and with greater security to your operations and
mine. I believe you cannot be too promptly nor too strongly
established on the Tennessee. I shall advance in a very few
days, as soon as our transportation is ready." On the 11th
the President issued War Order No. 3. "Major-General
McClellan, having personally taken the field at the head of
the Army of the Potomac, until otherwise ordered, he is relieved from the command of the other military departments,
he retaining command of the Department of the Potomac.

" Ordered further, that the two departments now under
the respective commands of Generals Halleck and Hunter,
together with so much of that, under General Buell, as lies
west of a north and south line indefinitely drawn through

Knoxville, Tennessee, be consolidated and designated the Department of the Mississippi; and that, until otherwise ordered, Major-General Halleck have command of said department." Immediately upon the receipt of this order, General Halleck ordered Buell to march his army to Savannah. The forces of the Confederacy were gathering at Corinth; the forces of Halleck and Buell were massing at Savannah. Instead of a hurried dash by a flying column, to tear up a section of railway as ancillary to a real movement elsewhere, the programme now contemplated a struggle by armies for the retention or for the destruction of a strategic point deemed almost vital to the Confederacy.

About the close of February, General Beauregard sent a field-battery, supported by two regiments of infantry, to occupy the river-bluff at Pittsburg Landing, twenty-three miles northwest from Corinth, and nine miles above Savannah. Lieutenant-Commander Gwin, who was stationed at Savannah with two gunboats, the Tyler and the Lexington, proceeded to Pittsburg Landing, on March 1st, and, after a brisk skirmish, silenced the battery and drove it and its supports away. General C. F. Smith, in pursuance of the authority given him by General Halleck, selected this as the point of assembly of the army.

Lick Creek, above the landing, and Snake Creek, below it, empty into the river about three miles apart, the landing being nearer the mouth of Snake Creek. Lick Creek, rising in a swamp, flows eleven miles nearly northeast to the river. Snake Creek flows nearly east to the river. Owl Creek flows nearly parallel to Lick Creek, at a distance from it varying from three to five miles, and empties into Snake Creek something more than a mile from its mouth. The land enclosed between these creeks and the river is a rolling plateau from eighty to a hundred feet above the river-level. The riverfront of this plateau is cut by sundry sloughs and ravines, which were at that time overflowed by back-water. One of these deep ravines, running back at right angles to the river, is immediately above the bluff at the landing. About a mile back from the river, and about a mile above the landing, is a swell in the ground, not marked enough to be called a ridge. From this higher ground extend the head ravines of Oak Creek,* a rivulet or brook flowing to the west, passing within a few hundred yards of Shiloh Church, and then turning to the northwest and flowing into Owl Creek. In the reports of Sherman's division this rivulet is treated as the main branch of Owl Creek, and called by that name. From the same rising ground, ravines, wet only after a rain, extend east and southeast to Lick Creek. From the same position extend the head ravines of Brier Creek,* a deep ravine with little water, which flows almost due north and empties into Snake Creek a little below the mouth of Owl Creek. The three principal creeks, Lick, Snake, and Owl, flow through swampy valleys, bordered by abrupt bluffs. Oak Creek, from the neighborhood of Shiloh Church to its mouth, flows through a miry bottom bordered by banks of less height. The land was for the most part covered with timber, partly with dense undergrowth; in places were perhaps a dozen open fields containing about eighty acres each. A road, lying far enough back from the river to avoid the sloughs, led from the landing to Hamburg Landing, about six miles above. Another road from the landing crossed Brier Creek and Snake Creek just above their junction, and continued down the river to Crump's Landing. The road to Corinth forked near the landing, one branch of it passing by Shiloh Church, the

---

* The names Oak Creek and Brier Creek are obtained from Colonel Charles Whittlesey, who made a study of the field every day for two weeks succeeding the battle.

other keeping nearer to the river, but both reuniting five or six miles out. The position selected thus, gave ample room to camp an army, was absolutely protected on the sides of the river, Snake Creek, and Owl Creek, while from its south face a ridge gave open way to Corinth. The open way to Corinth was also an open way from Corinth to the landing. This accessible front could easily have been turned into a strong defence, by taking advantage of the rolling ground, felling timber, and throwing up slight earthworks. But the army had many things yet to learn, and the use of field fortification was one of them.

In pursuance of General C. F. Smith's instructions to occupy the landing strongly, General Sherman ordered General Hurlbut to disembark his division and encamp it at right angles to the road about a mile out. The Corinth road designated was the one lying nearer to the river. About half a mile beyond the position selected for the camp the road forks, one being the Corinth road running southwest, the other running nearly due west, passed about four hundred yards north of Shiloh Church, crossed Oak Creek and Owl Creek immediately above their junction, and continued to Purdy. General Hurlbut the same day issued a field order in minute detail, and the First and Second Brigades being all of the division at hand, marched to the prescribed point, Burrows' battery being posted at the road; the First Brigade at right angles with the road, with its left at the battery; the Third Brigade at right angles with the road, its right at Burrows' battery, and Mann's battery at its left. The Second Brigade, commanded by Colonel Veatch, subsequently arriving, camped to the rear and partially to the right of the First Brigade, so as almost to interlock with the camp of General C. F. Smith's division.

On the 18th, Sherman's division of four brigades landed,

and moved out a few days later to permanent camp. The Second Brigade, sent to watch some fords of Lick Creek, was posted in the fork of a cross-road running to Purdy from the Hamburg road. The Fourth Brigade, commanded by Colonel Buckland, camped with its left near Shiloh Church, and its color-line nearly at right angles with the Corinth road. The First Brigade, commanded by Colonel McDowell, went into camp to the right of Buckland, and was separated from him by a lateral ravine running into Oak Creek ; the camp was pitched between the Purdy road and the bluff-banks of Oak Creek. The Third Brigade, commanded by Colonel Hildebrand, was posted to the left of Shiloh Church, its right being near the church. Precision in camping was not exacted, and the left regiment of Colonel Hildebrand's Brigade, the Fifty-third Ohio, in order to enclose a fine spring of water within the brigade, pitched its camp about two hundred yards to the left and front of its next regiment (the Fifty-seventh Ohio), and was separated from the rest of the brigade by this distance and by a stream with swampy borders which emptied into Oak Creek. General Sherman's headquarters were to the rear of Shiloh Church. His batteries, Taylor's and Waterhouse's, together with his cavalry, were camped in rear of the infantry.

General Grant arrived at Savannah on the 17th and assumed command, reported to General Halleck, and on the same day ordered General C. F. Smith's division to Pittsburg Landing. His division, the Second, encamped, not in a line, but in convenient localities on the plateau between Brier Creek and the river. McClernand with the First Division was sent a few days later, and selecting the most level ground, laid out the most regular camp. His front crossed the Corinth road about two-thirds of a mile in rear of Shiloh Church, the road intersecting his line near his left flank ;

the direction of his line was to the north-west, reaching
toward the bluffs of the valley of Snake Creek.   General
Prentiss reported to General Grant for assignment to duty,
and about March 25th, six new regiments, not yet assigned,
reported to him and were by him put into two brigades constituting the Sixth Division.   These brigades were subsequently increased by regiments assigned to him as late as
April 5th and 6th.   The Fifth Ohio Battery, Captain Hickenlooper, arriving on April 5th, was assigned to the Sixth
Division, and went into camp.   Prentiss' camp faced to the
south.   It is not easy now to identify precisely its position.
It appears incidentally, from reports of the battle of April
6th, that a ravine ran along the rear of the right of the
division camp, and another ravine in front of the left.   The
left regiment (the Sixteenth Wisconsin) of the right brigade
(Peabody's) lay on the lower or most southern branch of
the Corinth road ; the left flank of the division was in sight
of Stuart's brigade ; there was a considerable gap between
its right flank and Sherman's division.   The divisions were
not camped with a view to defence against an apprehended
attack ; but they did fulfil General Halleck's instructions to
General C. F. Smith, to select a depot with a view to the
march on to Corinth.   Sherman's division lay across one
road to Corinth, with McClernand's in its rear ; Prentiss' division lay across the other road to Corinth, with Hurlbut in
his rear, and C. F. Smith was camped so as to follow either.
The divisions did not march to the selected ground and
pitch camp in a forenoon ; but, partly from the rain and
mud, partly want of practice, some of the divisions were
several days unloading from the boats, hauling in the great
trains then allowed to regiments (twenty-seven wagons and
two ambulances to a regiment in some cases,) laying out the
ground, and putting up tents.   General Sherman, before set-

tling down in his camp, made a reconnoissance out to Monterey, nearly half way to Corinth, and dislodged a detachment of hostile cavalry camped there. Every division and many of the brigades found a separate drill-ground in some neighboring field, and constant drilling was preparing the command for the march to Corinth.

Major-General C. F. Smith received an injury to his leg by jumping into a yawl early in March. This injury, seeming trivial at first, resulted in his death on April 25th. It became so aggravated by the end of March that he was obliged to move from Pittsburg Landing to Savannah, leaving Brigadier-General W. H. L. Wallace in command of his division, and Major-General McClernand, senior officer present, at Pittsburg. General Grant—who went up from Savannah every day to visit the camps, and was requested by General McClernand, by letter on March 27th, to move his headquarters to Pittsburg Landing—was about to transfer his headquarters thither on April 4th, when he received a letter from General Buell saying he would arrive next day at Savannah, and requesting an interview. The transfer of headquarters was accordingly postponed till after the interview.

General L. Wallace's division disembarked at Crump's Landing on the same side of the river with Pittsburg Landing, and a little above Savannah. His First Brigade went into camp near the river ; the Second at Stony Lonesome, about two miles out on the road to Purdy ; the Third Brigade immediately beyond Adamsville, on the same road. The Third Brigade went into camp on the inner slope of a sharp ridge, and cut down the timber on the exterior slope, to aid the holding of the position in case of an attack in front.

While Grant's army was sailing up the river and getting settled at Pittsburg, General Buell with five divisions of his army was marching from Nashville to Savannah.   Immediately on receiving General Halleck's order to march, he sent out his cavalry to secure the bridges on his route, in which they succeeded, except in the cases of the important bridge over Duck Creek at Columbia, and an unimportant bridge a few miles north of that.   On the 15th, the Fourth Division, commanded by Brigadier-General A. McD. McCook, moved out, and at intervals, up to March 20th, it was followed in order by the Fifth, Brigadier-General T. L. Crittenden, Sixth, Brigadier-General T. J. Wood, and First, Brigadier-General George H. Thomas—37,000 men in all. Having no pontoons, General Buell built a bridge over Duck Creek.   This would have caused little delay later in the war; but to fresh troops, who yet had to learn the business of military service, it was a formidable task, and was not completed till the 29th.   While waiting for the completion of the bridge, General Buell's command learned that General Grant's army was on the west bank of the Tennessee.   General Nelson at once asked permission to ford the stream and push rapidly on to Savannah.   Permission being obtained, the division, with Ammen's brigade—the Twenty-fourth Ohio, Sixth Ohio, and Thirty-sixth Indiana in front—began their march early on the morning of the 29th, the men stripped of their pantaloons, carrying their cartridge-boxes on their necks ; the ammunition-boxes of the artillery taken from the limbers and carried over on scows, and tents packed in the bottom of the wagon-beds, to lift ammunition and stores above water.

The bridge was finished and the march resumed the same day.   Nelson having secured the advance, his eagerness gave an impetus to the entire column.   The divisions were ordered to camp at night six miles apart, making a column thirty miles long.   But this prevented the clogging

of the march on the wet and soft roads, the alternate crowd-
ing up and lengthening out of the column, the weary waiting
of the crowded rear for the obstructed front to move, nights
spent on the road, and late bivouacs reached toward morning.   It made Buell's advance slow, but it prevented the
new troops from being worn out, and brought them in good
condition onto the field.   General Buell intended to take
at Waynesboro the road to Hamburg Landing, instead of
the direct road to Savannah, and put his army there into a
separate camp.   General Nelson, however, moving faster
than was expected, drew the divisions behind him through
Waynesboro, on the road to Savannah, before General Buell
issued the order, and so unconsciously defeated the intention.   Nelson's brigade reached Savannah during April 5th,
Crittenden's division camped that night a few miles distant,
and General Buell himself reached Savannah or its outskirts
some time in the evening.

General A. S. Johnston was encamped with his army at
Edgefield, opposite Nashville, on February 15th. A despatch
from General Pillow that evening announced a great victory
won by the garrison of Fort Donelson.   Just before daybreak of the 16th another despatch was received, that Buckner would capitulate at daylight.   Immediately staff and
orderlies were aroused, and the troops put in motion across
the river to Nashville.   The morning papers were filled with
the "victory, glorious and complete," and the city was ring-
ing with joy. In the forenoon the news spread of the surrender of Donelson.   The people were struck with dismay,
the city was in panic, the populace was delirious with excitement.   A wild mob surrounded Johnston's headquarters
and demanded to know whether their generals intended to
fight or not.

Johnston immediately began the abandonment of Nash-

ville. First were sent off the fifteen hundred sick brought
on from Bowling Green, together with the tenants of the
hospitals at Nashville. The railway was then taxed to its
utmost to carry away the stores of most value. It was evident that all the stores could not be taken away, and pillage
of commissary stores and quartermaster stores by citizens
was permitted. A regiment of infantry and a battalion of
cavalry were put on guard and patrolled the streets to re-
duce the riotous to order. Johnston moved out with his
command on February 18th, leaving Floyd and Forrest with
a force in Nashville to preserve order, remove the public
stores, and to destroy what could not be removed.

Popular excitement always demands a victim, and the out-
cry was almost universal that Johnston should be relieved
from command. But, to a deputation that went to Jefferson
Davis, President of the Confederacy, with this request, he
replied : "I know Johnston well. If he is not a general, we
had better give up the war, for we have no general." Johnston found the Tennessee, running from Alabama and Mississippi up to the Ohio, in the possession of the National
fleets and armies. The force under his immediate command
was therefore separated from the force under Beauregard
that was guarding the Mississippi. Unless they should join,
they would be beaten in detail. To join involved the surrender either of Central Tennessee or of the Mississippi.
Johnston resolved to give up Central Tennessee until he
could regain it, and hold on to the Mississippi. But to hold
the Mississippi required continued possession of the railroads, and such points especially as Corinth and Humboldt.
Corinth, both from its essential importance and its exposure
to attack by reason of its nearness to the river, was the point
for concentration. Johnston moved from Nashville to Murfreesboro, not on the direct route to Corinth, to conceal his

purpose. At Murfreesboro he added to the forces brought
from Bowling Green between three and four thousand of
the men who escaped from Donelson, and the command of
General Crittenden from Kentucky, quickly raising his force
at Murfreesboro to seventeen thousand men.   Leaving Murfreesboro on February 28th, marching through Shelbyville to
Decatur, he arrived at Corinth, on March 24th, with twenty
thousand men.   General Bragg, with ten thousand well-
drilled troops from Pensacola, had preceded him.   General
Ruggles, with a brigade, came from New Orleans ; Major-
General Polk, with General Cheatham's division from Columbus, with the troops that escaped from Island No. Ten
the night before escape was cut off, and various outlying
garrisons under General Beauregard's command, swelled the
concourse. Van Dorn, having failed to drive Curtis back
into Missouri, was ordered to come with his command to
Corinth. A regiment arrived before April 6th, the rest later.
Detached commands guarding the line of the Memphis and
Charleston Railroad were called in. The governors of States
were called on and raised new levies. Beauregard made a
personal appeal for volunteers, which brought in several
regiments. Johnston had before called for reinforcements
in vain. Now every nerve was strained to aid him. An in-
spection of his command satisfied him that if all the soldiers
detailed as cooks and teamsters were relieved, he would have
another brigade of effective men.   He sent messengers
through the surrounding country, urging citizens to hire
their negroes as cooks and teamsters for ninety days, or even
sixty days.   But the messengers returned with the answer
that the planters would freely give their last son, but they
would not part with a negro or a mule.

  General Bragg, on arriving at Corinth, wished to attack
the troops as they were beginning to land at Pittsburg and

Crump's landings. General Beauregard forbade this, writing to Bragg: " I would prefer the defensive-offensive—that is, to take up such a position as would compel the enemy to develop his intentions, and to attack us, before he could penetrate any distance from his base; then, when within striking distance of us, to take the offensive and crush him wherever we may happen to strike him, cutting him off, if possible, from his base of operations or the river."

On March 25th, Johnston completed the concentration of his troops. Van Dorn was in person in Corinth, and was ordered to bring forward his command. Johnston determined to wait as long as practicable for it. Meanwhile, to hasten the organization and preparation of his army, he appointed Gen. Bragg chief of staff for the time, but to resume command of his corps when the movement should begin. Of him, Colonel William Preston Johnston says, in his life of his father—a valuable book, prepared with great industry, and written with an evident desire to be fair : " In Bragg there was so much that was strong marred by most evident weakness, so many virtues blemished by excess or defect in temper and education, so near an approach to greatness and so manifest a failure to attain it, that his worst enemy ought to find something to admire in him, and his best friend something painful in the attempt to portray him truly." A thorough disciplinarian and a master of detail, his merits found full play, and his defects were less apparent in his position on the staff.

Johnston was organizing his army ; Grant was assembling his twenty-three miles away. On the other side of the Tennessee, ninety miles from Savannah, Buell, halted by Duck Creek, was building a bridge for his troops — a bridge which it required twelve days to construct. Johnston having completed his concentration, it was his obvious policy to

attack before Grant should be further reinforced. General
Beauregard, in his letter of March 18th to Bragg, said:
"While I have guarded you against an uncertain offensive,
I am decidedly of the opinion that we should endeavor to
entice the enemy into an engagement as soon as possible,
and before he shall have further increased his numbers by
the large numbers which he must still have in reserve and
available—that is, beat him in detail." Lee wrote to Johnston, on March 26th : "I need not urge you, when your army
is united, to deal a blow at the enemy in your front, if possible, before his rear gets up from Nashville. You have him
divided, and keep him so, if you can." It was Johnston's
purpose, and expressed, to attack Grant before Buell should
arrive. But he determined to continue organizing and waiting for Van Dorn as long as that would be safe.

At eleven o'clock at night of April 2d, Johnston learned
that Buell was moving "rapidly from Columbia, by Clifton,
to Savannah." About one o'clock in the morning of Thursday, the 3d, preliminary orders were issued to hold the troops
in readiness to move at a moment's notice, with five days'
rations and one hundred rounds of ammunition. The movement began in the afternoon. The army was arranged in
three corps, commanded respectively by Polk, Bragg, and
Hardee, and a reserve under Breckenridge. Beauregard was
second in command, without a specific command. Major-
General Hardee's corps consisted of Brigadier-General Hindman's division and Brigadier-General Cleburne's brigade.
The division consisted of Hindman's brigade, commanded
by Colonel Shaver, and Brigadier-General Wood's brigade.
Wood's brigade comprised five regiments, and two battalions
of infantry and a battery ; Cleburne's brigade was composed
of six regiments and two batteries. Major-General Bragg's
corps consisted of two divisions, commanded respectively by

Brigadier-General Ruggles and Brigadier-General Withers. The brigades of Ruggles' division were commanded by Colonel Gibson, Brigadier-General Patton Anderson, and Colonel Pond. Withers' brigades were commanded by Brigadier-Generals Gladden, Chalmers, and Jackson. The brigades of Chalmers and Gladden contained each five regiments and a battery ; the other brigades contained each four regiments and a battery, with, in Anderson's and Pond's each, an additional battalion of infantry. Major-General Polk's corps had two divisions, commanded by Brigadier-General Clark and Major-General Cheatham. Clark's brigades were commanded by Colonel Russell and Brigadier-General A. P. Stewart ; Cheatham's brigades were commanded by Brigadier-General B. R. Johnson and Colonel Stephens. Each brigade was made up of four regiments of infantry and a battery. Brigadier-General John C. Breckenridge's reserve comprised three brigades, commanded by Colonel Trabue, Brigadier-General Bowen, and Colonel Statham. Trabue had five regiments and two battalions, Bowen four regiments, and Statham six regiments of infantry. Each brigade had a battery. By the returns, Cleburne's brigade was the largest, having 2,750 effectives. Besides, were three regiments, two battalions and one company of cavalry. This force comprised 40,000 of the 50,000 effectives gathered at Corinth. Different returns vary a few hundred more and a few hundred less. General Johnston telegraphed to Jefferson Davis, when the movement began, that the number was 40,000. In forming for battle, the army was to deploy into three parallel lines, the distance between the lines to be one thousand yards. Hardee's corps to be the first ; Bragg's the second ; and the third to be composed of Polk on the left and Breckenridge on the right.

Hardee, moving out in advance, in the afternoon of Thurs-

day, halted Friday forenoon at Mickey's house, about seventeen miles from Corinth.   Bragg's corps bivouacked Friday
night in rear of Hardee.   Clark's division of Polk's corps
followed in due order on its road.   Cheatham's division, on
outpost on the railroad at Purdy and Bethel, under orders
to defend himself if attacked, otherwise to assemble at
Purdy, march thence to Monterey, and thence to position
near Mickey's, did not leave Purdy till Saturday morning,
and reached his position Saturday afternoon.   Breckenridge,
who marched from his station at Burnesville through Farmington without entering Corinth, using a cross-road, could
not pull his wagons through the mud, and failed to get as
far as Monterey Friday night.   While Hardee was lying near
Mickey's house, his cavalry felt the National outposts, and
a reconnoitring party from the National camp struck Cleburne's brigade.

The order issued at Corinth required the columns to be
deployed by seven o'clock, Saturday morning, and the attack
to begin at eight o'clock.   Hardee began his movement at
daybreak, Saturday, deployed about ten o'clock, and waited.
His line being too short to extend from Owl Creek to Lick
Creek, Gladden's brigade was moved forward from Bragg's
corps, and added to Hardee's right.   The rest of Withers'
division moved into position behind Hardee's right; but
Ruggles' division, constituting the right of Bragg's line, did
not appear.   Successive messengers bringing no satisfaction,
General Johnston rode to the rear with his staff, till he found
Ruggles' division standing still, with its head in an open
field.   It was set in motion, Polk followed; Cheatham arrived
from Purdy; Breckenridge extricated his command from the
deep mud, and, by four o'clock in the afternoon, the deployment and formation of the army was complete.   It was too
late to attack that day.   Beauregard urged that it was too

late to attack at all, that it would now be impossible to effect a surprise, that the expedition should be abandoned and the troops march back to Corinth. Johnston directed the troops to bivouac, and attack to be made next day at daylight.

Of the five divisions at Pittsburg Landing, the organization of four—the First, McClernand's; Second, C. F. Smith's, commanded by Brigadier-General W. H. L. Wallace, General Smith being ill at Savannah; the Fourth, Hurlbut's; and the Fifth, Sherman's—was completed. The Sixth, commanded by Prentiss, was still in process of formation. McClernand's First Brigade, composed of the Eighth and Eighteenth Illinois, Eleventh and Thirteenth Iowa, was commanded by Colonel Hare, of the Eleventh Iowa; the Second was composed of the Eleventh, Twentieth, Forty-fifth, and Forty-eighth Illinois, and commanded by Col. Marsh, of the Twentieth Illinois; the Third, of the Seventeenth, Twenty-ninth, Forty-third, and Forty-ninth Illinois. Colonel Ross, of the Seventeenth Illinois, the senior colonel, being ill and absent, the command of this brigade devolved on Colonel Reardon, of the Twenty-ninth. The Second Division comprised three brigades: the First, commanded by Colonel Tuttle, of the Second Iowa, contained the Second, Seventh, Twelfth, and Fourteenth Iowa; the Second, commanded by Brigadier-General McArthur, comprised the Thirteenth and Fourteenth Missouri, Ninth and Twelfth Illinois, and Eighty-first Ohio. The Fourteenth Missouri, at that time, went by the name of Birge's Sharpshooters; the Third, commanded by Colonel Sweeney, of the Fifty-second Illinois, comprised the Eighth Iowa, and the Seventh, Fiftieth, Fifty-second, Fifty-seventh, and Fifty-eighth Illinois. The Fourth Division contained three brigades: the First, commanded by Colonel Williams, of the Third Iowa, contained the Third Iowa, Twenty-eighth, Thirty-second, and Forty-first Illinois; the Second, commanded by Colonel Veatch, of the Twenty-fifth Indiana, con-

tained the Twenty-fifth Indiana, Fourteenth, Fifteenth, and
Forty-sixth Illinois; the Third, commanded by Brigadier-
General Lauman, who reported for duty Saturday, April 5th,
and was then assigned to this command, comprised the
Thirty-first and Forty-fourth Indiana, and the Seventeenth
and Twenty-fifth Kentucky. The Fifth Division contained
four brigades: the First, commanded by Colonel McDowell,
of the Sixth Iowa, was made of the Sixth Iowa, Forty-sixth
Ohio, and the Fortieth Illinois; the Second, commanded by
Colonel Stuart, of the Fifty-fifth Illinois, was made of the
Fifty-fifth Illinois and the Fifty-fourth and Seventy-first
Ohio; the Third, commanded by Colonel Hildebrand, of the
Seventy-seventh Ohio, contained the Fifty-third, Fifty-sev-
enth, and Seventy-seventh Ohio; the Fourth, commanded by
Colonel Buckland, of the Seventy-second Ohio, contained the
Forty-eighth, Seventieth, and Seventy-second Ohio.   The
Sixth Division was organized into two brigades: the First
Brigade, commanded by Colonel Peabody, of the Twenty-fifth
Missouri, contained the Twenty-first and Twenty-fifth Mis-
souri, Twelfth Michigan, and Sixteenth Wisconsin.   The
Second, commanded by Colonel Miller, of the Eighteenth
Missouri, comprised the Eighteenth Missouri and Sixty-first
Illinois.   The Sixteenth Iowa, assigned to this brigade, arriving fresh from the recruiting depot, without ammunition,
on April 5th, reported to General Prentiss that day, but was
sent by him to the landing early in the morning of the 6th,
and was by General Grant assigned to duty that day in another part of the field.   The Eighteenth Wisconsin arrived
and reported on April 5th, and the Twenty-third Missouri
arrived in the morning of the 6th, and reported on the field
at nine o'clock.*   But these two regiments were not formally

---

* The Fifteenth Michigan arriving without ammunition, immediately before the
attack began, marched to the rear for ammunition and, returning to the field, fought
through the day between the Eighteenth Missouri and the Eighteenth Wisconsin.

assigned to either brigade. The Fifteenth Iowa, assigned to this division, arrived the morning of April 6th, and was assigned to duty in another part of the field. The Fourteenth Wisconsin, assigned to the division, arrived late in the night of April 6th, and served on the 7th with Crittenden's division of Buell's army.

The artillery was not attached to brigades, but was under the direct command of division commanders. The batteries of Schwartz and McAllister, and Burrow's Fourteenth Ohio Battery served with McClernand's division. Willard's Company A, First Illinois Artillery, commanded by Lieutenant Wood, and Major Cavender's battalion of Companies D, H, and I, First Missouri Artillery, were attached to W. H. L. Wallace's division. Mann's four-gun battery, Ross' Second Michigan, and Myer's Thirteenth Ohio batteries, were attached to Hurlbut's division. Behr's Sixth Indiana Battery, and Barrett's Company B, and Waterhouse's Company E, First Illinois Artillery, were attached to Sherman's division. Barrett's battery had formerly been commanded by Captain Ezra Taylor, promoted Major of the First Illinois Artillery, and was still commonly called Taylor's battery, and is so styled in some of the reports of the battle. Munch's Minnesota and Hickenlooper's Fifth Ohio Battery were attached to Prentiss' division. There was some change in the assignment of batteries on April 5th. The above gives their position as it was on April 6th. Bouton's Company I, First Illinois Artillery, and Dresser's battery, commanded by Captain Timony, though not assigned, were given positions on the field by Major Ezra Taylor, Sherman's chief of artillery, by direction of General Grant. Margraff's Eighth Ohio Battery served with Sherman, Powell's Company F, Second Illinois Artillery, served with Prentiss. Madison's Company B, Second Illinois Artillery, served at the landing. Captain Silversparre's four-gun battery of twenty-pound

Parrotts, though assigned to McClernand, remained at the landing from lack of horses and equipage to pull them out to camp.

The Third Division, commanded by General Lewis Wallace, comprised three brigades: The First Brigade, commanded by Colonel Morgan L. Smith, of the Eighth Missouri, comprising the Eleventh and Twenty-fourth Indiana and the Eighth Missouri, was in camp at Crump's Landing; the Second Brigade, commanded by Colonel Thayer, of the First Nebraska, comprising the First Nebraska, Twenty-third Indiana, and Fifty-eighth and Sixty-eighth Ohio, was camped at Stony Lonesome, two miles out from Crump's Landing; the Third Brigade, commanded by Colonel Whittlesey, of the Twentieth Ohio, comprising the Twentieth, Fifty-sixth, Seventy-sixth, and Seventy-eighth Ohio, was in camp at Adamsville, three miles out beyond Stony Lonesome, or five miles from Crump's Landing.   Buell's Battery I, First Missouri Artillery, commanded by Lieutenant Thurber, and Thompson's Ninth Indiana Battery, constituted the artillery of the division.

The cavalry consisted of the Fifth Ohio, Fourth and Eleventh Illinois, Companies A and B, Second Illinois, under Captain Houghtaling, two companies of regular cavalry under Lieutenant Powell, Stewart's battalion, and Thielman's battalion.   The Third Battalion of the Fifth Ohio and the Third Battlion of the Eleventh Illinois remained with Lewis Wallace. The rest of the cavalry was assigned to different divisions, but the assignment was changed on April 5th.

The Fifth Ohio Cavalry, attached to Sherman's division till April 5th, frequently made reconnoitring expeditions some miles to the front, and frequently encountered parties of hostile cavalry. Thursday, April 3d, General Sherman sent Buckland's brigade out on a reconnoissance on the

Corinth road, but with strict injunctions, in accordance with
General Halleck's repeated order, not to be drawn into a
fight with any considerable force of the enemy, that would
risk bringing on a general engagement.   Buckland marched
to the fork of the road about five miles out, which must have
been at Mickey's.   General Hardee states that Mickey's is
about eight miles from the landing.   Posting the brigade
between the roads, he sent two companies out on each road.
Both encountered hostile cavalry, understood to be pickets,
within half a mile, began skirmishing with them, and saw a
larger body of cavalry beyond. The companies were recalled,
and the brigade reached camp a little before dark and reported.   Next day, Friday, the 4th, a cavalry dash on Buckland's picket-line swooped off a lieutenant and seven men.
General Buckland, who was near, sent information to Sherman, who sent out 150 cavalry.   Major Crockett, who was
drilling his regiment near by, sent a company to scout beyond the picket-line.   Major Crockett was sent by General
Buckland with another company, to bring the first one back.
Before long firing was heard, Buckland started with a battalion to the rescue, found the second company had been attacked and Major Crockett captured, pushed on a distance
estimated at two miles, attacked unseen a body of cavalry just
about to charge upon the first company, was reinforced by
the cavalry sent out by Sherman, pursued the hostile cavalry
a distance estimated another mile, came in view of artillery
and infantry, was fired on by the artillery, returned bringing
in ten prisoners, and found General Sherman at the picket-
posts with a brigade in line.   The same evening, in obedience to an order from General Sherman, Buckland sent him
a written report.   This advance was the attack upon Cleburne's brigade reported by General Hardee.

Saturday the cavalry were moving camps, in obedience

to the order of reassignment. Batteries were moving about under the same order.   Buckland and Hildebrand anxiously visited their picket-lines and observed the parties of hostile cavalry hovering in the woods beyond.   Some of the men on picket claimed they had seen infantry.   Captain Mason of the Seventy-seventh Ohio, on picket, observed at daylight, Saturday morning, numbers of rabbits and squirrels scudding from the woods to and across his picket-line.   General Sherman was advised, but he had no cavalry to send out ; the Fifth had gone, and the Fourth not yet reported.   He enjoined Buckland and Hildebrand to be vigilant, strengthen their pickets, and be prepared for attack.   Additional companies were sent out to increase the pickets, Buckland established a connecting line of sentries from the picket reserve to camp, to communicate the first alarm on the picket-line, and instructed his officers to be prepared for a night attack.

Saturday afternoon, General Prentiss, in consequence of information received from his advance guard, sent Colonel Moore, of the Twenty-first Missouri, with three companies from his regiment, to reconnoitre the front.   The line of his march being oblique to the line of the camp, led him out beyond the front of Sherman's line.   He marched in that direction three miles, saw nothing, and returned to camp. The oblique direction of his march prevented his running into Hardee's lines.   Prentiss, assured there was some activity—a cavalry reconnoissance in his front—pushed his pickets out a mile and a half and reinforced them.   McClernand, the same day, went out with Colonel McPherson and a battalion of cavalry on a reconnoissance toward Hamburg and a short distance out on the road to Corinth, and saw a few hostile scouts back of Hamburg.

General Lewis Wallace's reconnoitring parties developed the presence of a considerable force at Purdy and Bethel,

on the railroad.   Getting information, Friday night, of signs
of preparation for movement by this force, an order was sent
to the brigade at Adamsville to form line at daybreak.   The
other brigades reached Adamsville at an early hour, and all
remained prepared to repel attack till noon.   The activity
observed at Purdy and Bethel was, in fact, Cheatham's preparation for his march, Saturday, to his position in General
Polk's line.   General Grant being advised, Friday, by L.
Wallace, of the assembling of the force in his front, directed
W. H. L. Wallace to hold his division in readiness to move
to the support of L. Wallace immediately in case he should
be threatened; and advised Sherman to instruct his pickets
to be on the alert, and to be ready to move in support with
his whole division, and with Hurlbut's if necessary, if an
attack on L. Wallace should be attempted.   W. H. L. Wallace and Sherman commanded, by their respective positions,
the bridges across Owl Creek, over which passed the two
roads from the camps at Pittsburg Landing to L. Wallace.

Saturday, Sherman wrote to Grant: "All is quiet along
my lines now.   We are in the act of exchanging cavalry,
according to your orders.   The enemy has cavalry in our
front, and I think there are two regiments of infantry and
one battery of artillery about six miles out.   I will send you
in ten prisoners of war, and a report of last night's affair, in
a few minutes.

"Your note is just received.   I have no doubt that nothing
will occur to-day, more than some picket-firing.   The enemy
is saucy, but got the worst of it yesterday, and will not press
our pickets far.   I will not be drawn out far, unless with certainty of advantage; and I do not apprehend anything like
an attack upon our position."   A little later in the day, General Sherman wrote to Grant: "I infer that the enemy is in
some considerable force at Pea Ridge [another name for

Monterey] ; that yesterday they crossed a bridge with two regiments of infantry, one regiment of cavalry, and one battery of field-artillery, to the ridge on which the Corinth road lays. They halted the infantry and artillery at a point about five miles in my front, and sent a detachment to the house of General Meeks, on the north of Owl Creek, and the cavalry down toward our camp. This cavalry captured a part of our advance pickets, and afterward engaged two companies of Colonel Buckland's regiment, as described by him in his report herewith enclosed. Our cavalry drove them back upon their artillery and infantry, killing many and bringing ten prisoners (all of the First Alabama Cavalry), whom I send you." General Grant on the same day despatched to General Halleck : "Just as my letter of yesterday to Captain McLean, Assistant Adjutant-General, was finished, notes from Generals McClernand's and Sherman's assistant adjutant-generals were received, stating that our outposts had been attacked by the enemy, apparently in considerable force. I immediately went up, but found all quiet. The enemy took two officers and four or five of our men prisoners, and wounded four. We took eight prisoners and killed several. Number of the enemy's wounded not known. They had with them three pieces of artillery, and cavalry and infantry. How much cannot, of course, be estimated. I have scarcely the faintest idea of an attack (general one) being made upon us, but will be prepared should such a thing take place. General Nelson's division has arrived. The other two, of Buell's column, will arrive to-morrow or next day. It is my present intention to send them to Hamburg, some four miles above Pittsburg, when they all get here. From that point to Corinth the road is good, and a junction can be formed with the troops from Pittsburg at almost any point. Colonel McPherson has gone with an escort to-day to examine the defensibility of the ground about Hamburg, and to lay out the position of the camp, if advisable to occupy that place." Earlier on the same day General Grant also telegraphed to General Halleck : " The main force of the enemy is at Corinth, with troops at different points east. Small garrisons are also at Bethel, Jackson, and Humboldt. The number at these places seems constantly to change. The number of the enemy at Corinth, and within supporting distance of it, cannot be far from eighty thousand men." General Halleck was preparing to leave St. Louis and come to the front to take immediate command of the combined army for the march on to Corinth. He advised Buell he would leave in the beginning of the coming week.

II.—6

CHAPTER VI.

THREE companies of the Twenty-fifth Missouri, which regiment formed the right of Colonel Peabody's brigade, Prentiss' division, were sent out on reconnoissance about three o'clock in the morning of Sunday, April 6th. Following the road cautiously in a south-westerly direction, oblique to the line of the camp, they struck the enemy's pickets in front of General Sherman's division. General Johnston, at breakfast with his staff, hearing the fire of the encounter, turned to Colonel Preston and to Captain Munford, and directed them to note the hour in their blank books. It was just fourteen minutes after five o'clock.

Order was given to advance. To communicate the order along the line required time. General Beauregard says the advance began at half-past five. The three companies struck a battalion under Major Hardcastle, on Hardee's picket-line. Major Hardcastle was posted on picket with a battalion of the Third Mississippi, a quarter of a mile in front of Wood's brigade, Hardee's corps. Lieutenant McNulty was posted with a small party, one hundred yards, and Lieutenant Hammock with another small party, two hundred yards, in front of the centre of the battalion. Cavalry videttes were still farther to the front. The Major reports: "About dawn, the cavalry videttes fired three shots, wheeled and galloped back. Lieutenant Hammock suffered the enemy to approach within ninety yards. Their line seemed to be three hundred and fifty yards long, and to number about one thousand. He fired upon them and joined his battalion with his men. Lieutenant McNulty received the enemy with his fire at about one hundred yards, and then joined his battalion with his men, when the videttes rode back to my main position. At the first alarm my men were in line and all ready. I was on a rise of ground, men kneeling. The enemy opened a heavy fire on us at a distance of about two hundred yards, but most of the shots passed over us. We returned the fire immediately and kept it up. Captain Clare, aide to General Wood, came and encouraged us. We fought the enemy an hour or more, without giving an inch. Our loss in this engagement was: killed, four privates; severely wounded, one sergeant, one corporal, and eight privates; slightly wounded, the color-sergeant and nine privates. At about 6.30 A.M. I saw the brigade formed in my rear, and I fell back."

At six o'clock, Colonel Moore, of the Twenty-first Missouri, also of Peabody's brigade, was directed by General Prentiss to move out with five companies to support the pickets. About half a mile from camp he met the three companies of the Twenty-fifth returning. Despatching the wounded on to camp, and sending for the rest of his regiment, he halted with the detachment of the Twenty-fifth till joined by his remaining five companies. So reinforced, he continued his advance three hundred yards, met the advance of Shaver's brigade, halted on the edge of a field, and repulsed it. Colonel Moore being wounded, Lieutenant-Colonel Van Horn took command, and was further reinforced; after an engagement of half an hour, was overpowered and fell back to the support of the brigade.

According to General Bragg's report, Johnston's line of battle, after marching less than a mile beyond the scene of the first attack made by the three companies of the Twenty-fifth Missouri, came upon the strengthened National pickets, which he calls advanced posts. These fell back fighting. The army advanced steadily another mile, pushing back the fighting pickets, and then encountered the National troops "in strong force almost along the entire line. His batteries were posted on eminences, with strong infantry supports. Finding the first line was now unequal to the work before it, being weakened by extension, and necessarily broken by the nature of the ground, I ordered my whole force to move up steadily and promptly to its support."

Thus opened the battle of Shiloh. A combat made up of numberless separate encounters of detached portions of broken lines, continually shifting position and changing direction in the forest and across ravines, filling an entire day, is almost incapable of a connected narrative. As the first shock of the meeting lines of battle was near the right of the National line, an intelligible account may be given by describing the action of the divisions of Grant's army separately, beginning with the right, or Sherman's.

The direction of General Johnston's advance was such as to bring him first in contact with Sherman's left and Prentiss's right. To preserve even an approximate alignment of a line of battle of two miles front, marching with artillery, through wet forest, over rough, yet soft ground, with regiments in column doubled on the centre, the advance was necessarily slow. The reports show that portions of the second line, instead of keeping the prescribed distance of eight hundred yards in rear of the first, overtook it, and had to halt to regain the distance. The National pickets, posted a mile in front of the camps, were struck about half-past six o'clock Colonel J. Thompson, aide-de-camp to General Beauregard, in his report to his chief, says : " The first can-

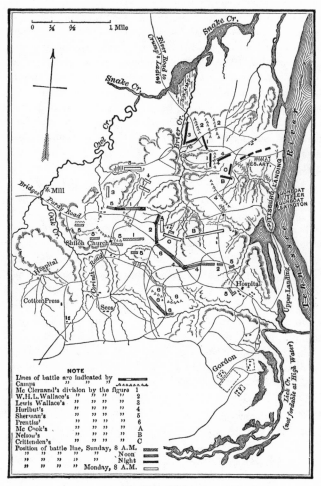

The Field of Shiloh.

non was discharged on our left at seven o'clock, which was followed by a rapid discharge of musketry. About 7.30 I rode forward with Colonel Jordan to the front, to ascertain how the battle was going. Then I learned from General Johnston that General Hardee's line was within half a mile of the enemy's camps, and bore from General Johnston a message that he advised sending forward strong reinforcements to our left. From eight o'clock to 8.30 the cannonading was very heavy along the whole line, but especially in the centre, which was in the line of their camps. About ten o'clock you moved forward with your staff and halted within about half a mile of the enemy's camps."

SHERMAN'S DIVISION.

The Seventy-seventh Ohio, of Hildebrand's brigade, was ordered the evening before to go out to See's, Sunday morning, and reinforce the picket reserve stationed there, and was up early Sunday morning. General Buckland, having slept little in the night, rose early. While at breakfast he received word that the pickets were heavily attacked, and were falling back toward camp. He at once had the long-roll sounded, and his brigade formed on the color-line. He rode over to General Sherman's headquarters, a few hundred yards off, and reported the facts. Meanwhile, the brigades of Hildebrand and McDowell formed on their respective color-lines. The division was formed—Taylor's battery on a rising ground in front of Shiloh Church; Hildebrand's brigade to its left, the Seventy-seventh Ohio being next to the battery, and four guns of Waterhouse's battery placed between the Fifty-seventh and Fifty-third Ohio—the Fifty-third detached and forming the extreme left. The other two guns of Waterhouse's battery were advanced to the front beyond Oak Creek. Buckland's brigade formed to the right of Taylor's battery, and McDowell's still farther to the right, on the bluffs of Oak Creek, near its junction with Owl Creek, and separated from Buckland by a lateral ravine which opened into Oak Creek. Behr's battery was with McDowell. One of its guns, with two companies of infantry, was stationed still farther to the right, commanding the bridges over Oak Creek and Owl Creek, immediately above their junction.

The advanced section of Waterhouse's battery fell back before an approaching skirmish line and took position with the battery. General Sherman rode to the front of the Fifty-third, to the edge of a ravine, the continuation or source of Oak Creek, and saw, through the forest beyond, Johnston's lines sweeping across his front toward his left. At the same time, General Johnston was, a few hundred yards off, on the other side of the ravine, putting General Hindman with one of his brigades into position for attack. Hindman's skirmishers opened fire and killed Sherman's orderly. Sherman's brigades advanced to the sloping of the ravine of Oak Creek; Sherman had already sent word to General McClernand asking for support to his left; to General Prentiss, giving him notice that the enemy was in force in front; and to General Hurlbut, asking him to suppport Prentiss.

The first line of Johnston's army, commanded by General Hardee, opened, widening the intervals between brigades as it advanced. The two brigades commanded by General Hindman, having less rough ground to traverse, outstripped General Cleburne. Hindman's own brigade, commanded by Colonel Shaver, inclining to the right, struck Prentiss' right. General Hindman in person, with Wood's brigade, came to the front of the Fifty-third Ohio. General Johnston, having put it in position, rode back to Cleburne and

moved his brigade to Buckland's front.   The battle opened.
The Fifty-third Ohio, detached by the position of its camp
from the rest of Hildebrand's brigade, being off to the left
and farther to the front, was first engaged.   According to
the report of Lieutenant-Colonel Fulton, the advancing line
of Wood's brigade having twice recoiled before the fire of
the regiment, Colonel Appler cried out to his men to fall
back and save themselves.   The regiment retired in confusion behind McClernand's Third Brigade, which had come
up in support; but, soon rallied by the Lieutenant-Colonel
and Adjutant Dawes, it returned to the front to the bank of
the stream.   The colonel reappeared and again ordered a
retreat.   The regiment was now fatally broken.   Adjutant
Dawes, however, rallied two companies and attached them to
the Seventeenth Illinois, of McClernand's Third Brigade,
while a considerable detachment joined the Seventy-seventh
Ohio, then commanded by Major Fearing.   In the afternoon,
Lieutenant-Colonel Fulton, with the greater part of the regiment reunited, acted as support to Bouton's battery.

General Patton Anderson, with his brigade, and Captain
Hodgson's battery of the Washington Artillery, pressed forward from Johnston's second line, commanded by General
Bragg, into the gap between Hindman and Cleburne.   Posting his battery on high ground, he advanced his brigade
down into the wet and bushy valley of Oak Creek, and
charged up the slope.   Taylor's battery and the Fifty-seventh and Seventy-seventh Ohio instantly drove him back.
His regiments, not discouraged, charged singly, and when
broken, charged by battalion, but could not withstand the
fire, and as often fell back.   General Johnston, who had
passed on toward his right, dispatched two brigades, Russell's and Johnson's, from the third line, commanded by
General Polk, to aid the assault.   General Beauregard

moved them to his right, beyond Hindman, to attack McClernand.

Meanwhile, Cleburne, forming the extreme left of Hardee's
line, with his brigade of six regiments and two batteries
engaged Buckland. The valley of Oak Creek is there wider,
deeper, and boggy. The slope, crowned by Buckland's brigade, was steep and bushy. A bend in its course gave some
companies of the Seventieth Ohio an enfilading fire. Cleburne's regiments, tangled in the morass, struggled with
uneven front up the wooded ascent, only to be driven back
by Buckland's steady fire. Reforming, they charged again,
to meet another repulse. The regiments, broken, disordered, and commingled, persisted in the vain endeavor, only
to encounter heavier losses. The Sixth Mississippi lost 300
killed and wounded out of a total of 425. More than one-
third of the brigade were killed and wounded. Pond's brigade, of Bragg's corps, came up in support, but paused on
the wooded bank, and did not attempt to cross this valley
of death.

McClernand's other brigades, which were to the left of the
Third, after some very sharp fighting, fell back. The long
line of Wood's brigade then largely outreached Colonel
Raith's left flank. Raith refused his left regiments. Wood's
brigade wheeled to their left, confronting Raith's new line.
Waterhouse's battery, being taken on the flank, was limbering
up to withdraw, when Major Taylor ordered it into action
again. Raith's regiments gave way. Wood's brigade charged
on Waterhouse's battery, capturing three of its guns. Captain
Waterhouse and two lieutenants being wounded, Lieutenant
Fitch, by order of Major Taylor, retired to the river with the
two pieces that were saved sound. The Fifty-seventh and
Seventy-seventh Ohio being now assailed on the flank by
Wood's advance, fell back in disorder. Anderson's brigade

9

then gathered itself up, emerged from the wet borders of
the creek, and gained the plateau in front of Hildebrand's
camps. Buckland's rear was now commanded by a hostile
battery and threatened by Wood's brigade. General Sherman at ten o'clock ordered his division to take position to
the rear along the Purdy road. Barrett's battery, moving
back by the Corinth road, came into position with Mc-
Clernand's division in its second position. McDowell's brigade had not yet been engaged, and to get into the new
position merely shifted his line to the left along the road.
Buckland moved back through his camp in order, his wagons
carrying off his dead and wounded and such baggage as they
could hold. The greater part of the Seventy-seventh Ohio,
commanded by Major Fearing, together with some companies of the Fifty-seventh, held by Lieutenont-Colonel
Rice, and some companies of the Fifty-third, represented
Hildebrand's brigade. Colonel Hildebrand finding his command so reduced, served part of the day on McClernand's
staff, but returned to General Sherman in the evening.
Colonel Crafts Wright, commanding the Thirteenth Missouri
in W. H. L. Wallace's division, was ordered in the morning
to take a designated position on the Purdy road. This
brought him on the left of General Sherman's new line.
The remnant of Hildebrand's brigade formed on Wright's
left and operated with him.

Meanwhile General Grant, at breakfast at Savannah, nine
miles below Pittsburg Landing by river, but six miles in an
air-line, heard the firing. He at once sent an order to General
Nelson to march his division up the river to opposite Pittsburg ; and, not aware that General Buell had arrived the previous evening, sent a letter out to meet him, advising him of
the order given to Nelson and explaining the reason for not
waiting in person for his arrival. Steaming up the river, he

stopped at Crump's Landing at eight o'clock and directed
Lewis Wallace to hold his division in readiness to move.
Arrived at Pittsburg Landing, Colonel Pride, of his staff, at
once organized ammunition trains, which were busy all day
supplying the troops at the front.   The Twenty-third Missouri, just arrived by boat, he hurried out to reinforce Prentiss.   The Fifteenth Iowa, just arrived, and the Sixteenth,
sent by Prentiss to the landing for ammunition, he directed
to form line, arrest the tide of stragglers from the front, and
organize them to return.   Riding to the front, he found
General Sherman a little before ten o'clock in his hottest
engagement, still holding the enemy at bay in front of his
camp; told him that Wallace would come up from Crump's
Landing; sent word to Wallace to move; to Nelson, to hasten his movements; returned to the landing, dispatched the
two Iowa regiments to reinforce McClernand, and proceeded
to visit the other divisions in the field.

The loaded wagons of McDowell's brigade, hurrying to the
rear along the Purdy road, interfered with the formation of
Sherman's new line.   Behr's battery, galloping to the position assigned to it—the centre of the line—added to the difficulty.   This battery was hardly in position and under fire
before Captain Behr was killed, and the men abandoned
their guns, fleeing from the field with the caissons.   The
line so disordered and broken was hard pressed by the enemy, and Sherman selected another line of defence, to his
left and rear, connecting with McClernand's right.   McDowell, nearly cut off by the enemy's pressing through the gap
left by Behr's men, brought the remaining gun of this battery from its position near the bridge, and by a rapid fire
pressed back the advance.   His regiments became separated
while struggling through dense thickets to the new position.
The Fortieth Illinois found itself marching by the flank,

with a deep ravine along its left, and a confederate regiment marching in parallel course not far to its right. Thus cut off, the Fortieth formed with its rear to the ravine, with a desperate effort drove its dangerous companion out of the way, and, pushing through the timber, came into a valley in rear of McClernand.

Not all the force engaged in the two hours' fight in front of Sherman's camp followed him to his new position. Cleburne had difficulty in reforming his shattered command. The remnant of the Sixth Mississippi marched to the rear under command of the senior surviving captain, disabled for further service. The fragment of the Twenty-Third Tennessee remaining near Cleburne was sent to the rear to hunt up the portions that had broken from it in the contest. Cleburne, proceeding for his other regiments, was stopped by General Hardee about noon, and directed to collect and bring into action the stragglers who were thronging in the captured camps. With the aid of cavalry he gathered up an unorganized multitude; but, finding he could do nothing with them, he resumed the search for his remaining regiments. About two o'clock he found the Fifth and Twenty-fourth Tennessee and Fifteenth Arkansas "halted under the brow of an abrupt hill." The Second Tennessee had moved to the rear, and did not rejoin the brigade during the battle. Cleburne was not again severely engaged during the day. Colonel Pond kept his brigade, in pursuance of General Bragg's order, watching the crossings of Owl Creek.

But the brigades of Anderson and Wood pressed on. Trabue's heavy brigade of five regiments, two battalions and two batteries, had been detached from the reserve at Beauregard's request for reinforcements, and sent by Johnston to his extreme left. Skirting Owl Creek, he came in full force upon Sherman's right flank, at half-past twelve o'clock. McDowell's two remaining regiments, the Sixth Iowa and Forty-sixth Ohio, were quickly moved to confront Trabue. The Forty-sixth Ohio was more alert in movement, and opened a hot fire before Trabue was completely deployed and in position. A steady combat through the timber and underbrush, and across the ravines, lasted an hour and a half. The Sixth Iowa lost 51 killed and 120 wounded; the Forty-sixth Ohio, losing fewer killed, but more wounded —34 killed, 150 wounded, and 52 taken prisoners—was quite shattered, and took no further part in the battle. Colonel Trabue's estimate of the character of the fighting at this point appears from his statement that his command in this encounter killed and wounded four or five hundred of the Forty-Sixth Ohio alone. It appears also from his report, which has never been officially published, but which is printed in the "History of the First Kentucky Brigade," that, of the 844 casualties in the brigade in the two days' battle, 534 were in the four regiments engaged in this encounter. Sherman readjusted his line, resting his right on a deep ravine running to Owl Creek, and keeping his left in connection with McClernand. Trabue was reinforced by General A. P. Stewart and part of his brigade, and a part of Anderson's brigade which had been resting in a ravine in the rear. The struggle lasted with varying intensity and alternate success.

There were charges and countercharges, ground was lost and regained ; but the general result was a recession of the battered division to the left and rear. About four o'clock, during a lull, Sherman moved his reduced command still farther in the same direction, and took position so as to cover the road by which Lewis Wallace was to arrive. Here, with an open field in front, he was not further molested, and here he bivouacked for the night. At this point, Captain

Hickenlooper, who had been engaged all day in the sturdy defence made by Prentiss, joined Sherman with his battery. Buckland, rejoined by the Seventieth Ohio, was ordered, late in the afternoon, to take his brigade to the bridge over Snake Creek, by which Lewis Wallace was expected. From this point the Forty-eighth Ohio marched to the landing for ammunition, and was there detained as a portion of the force supporting the reserve artillery till next morning. The bridge appearing free from risk, Buckland returned to the place of bivouac, constituting the right of Sherman's line. The Thirteenth Missouri became separated from the division in the last struggle, was incorporated for the night in Colonel Marsh's collection of regiments, constituting for the night McClernand's right. The position of the Thirteenth during the night was close by the headquarter tents of General McArthur, of W. H. L. Wallace's division. The Fifty-third Ohio bivouacked with the Eighty-first Ohio, in front of the camp of the Second Iowa, in Tuttle's brigade of W. H. Wallace's division. McDowell's brigade had disappeared from the division. Portions of the Fifty-seventh and Seventy-seventh Ohio, with Lieutenant-Colonel Rice and Major Fearing, were still with Sherman, and formed the left of his line in the bivouac.

MCCLERNAND.

The Forty-third Illinois, of McClernand's brigade, being out by permission, Sunday morning, to discharge their pieces, which had been loaded since they marched to the picket-line, Friday evening, distant firing was heard. This being reported to General McClernand, he sent an order to Colonel Reardon to hold the brigade in readiness for action. Colonel Reardon, being confined to bed by illness, directed Colonel

Raith to assume command. There was some delay in getting the brigade formed, owing to the sudden change of commanders and to the incredulity of the officers in some of the regiments as to the reality of an attack. The brigade being at length formed, advanced, and took position, with its right near Waterhouse's battery—its line making an angle with Sherman's line, so as to throw the left of the brigade upon and along Oak Creek. Colonel Marsh, of the Twentieth Illinois, heard considerable musketry on the left of the National camp. This continuing without material interruption for some time, he ordered regimental commanders to be in readiness to form, and soon after received an order from General McClernand to form the brigade. Soon after the brigade was formed an order was received to advance to the support of General Sherman, who was reported to be heavily attacked. The brigade moved to the left to a position assigned by General McClernand. The First Brigade was ordered to form three regiments on the left of the Second, and to post one regiment, the Eleventh Iowa, in reserve in rear of the right of Colonel Marsh's brigade. The alignment of the Third Brigade, by Colonel Raith throwing his left too far to the front, so as to be exposed to a flank attack and also to cover Colonel Marsh's right, Colonel Raith wheeled his left to the rear to connect with Marsh. The right of McClernand's division, as thus formed, connected with Sherman, but the left was uncovered.

General Johnston sent two brigades from Polk's corps, Colonel Russell's and General B. R. Johnson's, to reinforce his extreme left. General Beauregard, who had taken immediate command on the Confederate left, sent them farther to his right, and they went into position on the left of Wood's brigade. Two regiments of Russell's brigade formed on the left of Wood; the rest were marched by General

Clark, the division commander, still farther to the right. Three of General Johnson's regiments formed on the right of Russell's two, while General Bragg moved Johnson's remaining two regiments off to his right, to another attack. The assault on Colonel Marsh was made with great fury. In five minutes most of the field officers in the brigade were killed or wounded. The enemy's fire seemed especially directed at Burrow's battery, posted in the centre of Marsh's brigade, all the horses of which were killed or disabled. The colonel and lieutenant-colonel of the Forty-eighth Illinois being wounded and taken off the field, the regiment finally became disorganized and retired in disorder. The other regiments fell back. The battery was lost. The first brigade, which had not been severely engaged, next retired in some disorder. The Third Brigade, being now enfiladed and turned on its left flank, Colonel Raith refused his left regiment, and was himself soon mortally wounded. Wood's brigade then wheeling to its left and advancing, the Third Brigade fell back, leaving Waterhouse's battery on the flank of Sherman's division exposed.

The division formed again, its right connected with Sherman's left on the Purdy road. When Sherman fell back from the Purdy road, McClernand adjusted his right to connect again with Sherman's left. While his right connected still with Sherman, his left for a while almost joined W. H. L. Wallace in the position which he had assumed, and, when pushed back still farther, his left was yet to some extent protected by the character of the ground, rough, intersected by ravines, and dotted with impenetrable thickets that intervened between it and W. H. L. Wallace. McAllister's battery, and Schwartz's battery commanded by Lieutenant Nispel, were reinforced by Taylor's battery, commanded by Captain Barrett, brought over from Sherman, and by Dresser's battery, commanded by Captain Timony.

A determined and desperate struggle ensued, which lasted, with occasional intermissions, till late in the afternoon. Shaver's brigade, which, after a severe and protracted contest, had overcome Peabody's brigade of Prentiss' division, was ordered to the attack upon the left of McClernand's line. Advancing across a wide and open field, he encountered so hot a fire in front and on his right flank, that his brigade recoiled back to the shelter of timber and halted paralyzed, till later in the day he was ordered to attack in another quarter.   General B. R. Johnson was wounded, and his brigade so severely handled that it retreated from the field, leaving its battery, Polk's, behind.   McClernand's whole division advanced in line, pushing the enemy back half a mile through and beyond his camp.   This success was only temporary.   Changing front to meet fresh attacks, refusing first one flank, then the other, clinging desperately to his camp, but, on the whole, shifting slowly back from one position to another, he formed, in the afternoon, in the edge of timber on the border of an open field, and here, during a pause of half an hour, supplied his command with ammunition.   The respite was followed by a more furious assault.   Falling back from his camp toward the river, to the farther side of a deep ravine running north and south, being the continuation of the valley or ravine of Brier Creek, he formed his line, facing west with wings refused, the centre being the apex, and still connecting on the right with the remnant of Sherman's division.   Several fitful onslaughts at intervals forced McClernand to refuse his left still farther.

The swinging around of McClernand's left, while he receded in a general direction toward the northeast, left a wide interval between his command and W. H. L. Wallace.   The force which had been massed against him and Sherman had been diminished by detachments sent to aid in the attack againt W. H. L. Wallace and Prentiss. The remainder drifted through the gap to Wallace's rear. Pond's brigade, to which had been assigned the special duty of guarding along Owl Creek against any advance around Johnston's left flank, constituted the extreme Confederate left. This brigade had been very little under fire during the day. The battery attached to it, Ketchum's, was now detached to aid in the assault upon Wallace's front. Pond, with three Louisiana regiments of his brigade, was directed to move to the left along the deep ravine which McClernand had crossed, and silence one of McClernand's batteries. Trabue's brigade, which had been struggling through the tangled forest covering rough ground, separated by a lateral ravine from the ground in rear of Wallace and Prentiss, through the dense thickets of which ravine no command had been able to penetrate, was just emerging from the forest, and crossing the Brier Creek ravine toward Hurlbut's camp. Trabue's men, catching sight of the blue uniform of Pond's Louisiana regiments, fired upon them. This being silenced, Pond's brigade continued down the ravine, and up a lateral ravine toward the river, Colonel Mouton's Eighteenth Louisiana in advance. As they neared the position the battery withdrew, unmasking a line of infantry. A murderous fire was opened by this line. Pond's brigade faltered, recoiled, withdrew ; the Eighteenth Louisiana, according to Colonel Mouton's report, leaving 207 dead and wounded in the ravine.

This was the final attack on the National right. But scarcely was this over before Hurlbut's command came falling back through his camp, pushed on by Bragg and Breckenridge. W. H. L. Wallace's regiments, finding the force which had been contending with Sherman and McClernand closing on their rear, faced about and fought to their rear ; some regiments succeeded in cutting their way through and streamed toward their camp. This sudden, tumultuous uproar, far in the rear of the day's conflict, infected McClernand's command, and a large part of it broke in disorder. The broken line was partially rallied and moved back to what McClernand designates as his eighth position taken in the course of the day, and here he bivouacked for the night, his right joining the left of Sherman's bivouac; the left swung back so as to make an acute angle with it. Colonel Marsh formed the right of the line. His "command having been reduced to a merely nominal one" in the afternoon, he had been sent back across the Brier Creek ravine before the rest of the division, to form a new line, arrest all stragglers, and detain all unattached fragments. Colonel Davis, with the Forty-sixth Illinois, was resting in front of their camp in Veatch's brigade, Hurlbut's division, but on Colonel Marsh's request took position on Marsh's right; McClernand, when he fell back, formed the rest of his command on Marsh's left. The line consisted of the Forty-sixth, Forty-eighth, Twentieth, Seventeenth, Forty-ninth, Forty-third, and Forty-fifth Illinois, the Thirteenth Missouri, and the Fifty-third and Eighty-first Ohio. The Forty-sixth Illinois lay in front of its camp, being the right of Veatch's brigade camp, Hurlbut's division. The Forty-eighth and Twentieth lay on its left. The Seventeenth, Forty-ninth, and Forty-third moved around to connect with Sherman's left. The position of the Forty-third was between the bivouac of the Forty-sixth Illinois and the Thirteenth Missouri, and midway between the camp of the Ninth Illinois of McArthur's brigade, W. H. L. Wallace's division, and the camp of the Forty-sixth Illinois. The Fifty-third and Eighty-first Ohio were in front of the camp of the Second Iowa, Tuttle's Brigade, W. H. L. Wallace's division. Colonel Crocker, Thirteenth Iowa, who had assumed command of the First Brigade on the wounding of Colonel Hare, bivouacked with his regiment in front of the camp of the Fourteenth Iowa, Tuttle's brigade. The Eighth and Eighteenth Illinois spent the night with the reserve artillery.

Colonel Veatch, commanding Hurlbut's Second Brigade, formed his command at half-past seven o'clock in the morning, and was shortly after ordered to march to the support of Sherman. He reached a point not well defined, between nine and ten o'clock, and was placed in reserve. He soon became hotly engaged on McClernand's left. His two right regiments, the Fifteenth and Forty-sixth Illinois, became separated from Colonel Veatch with the other two regiments, and then separated from each other. The Forty-sixth aided the Sixth Iowa and Forty-sixth Ohio in their desperate struggle with Trabue, and after continual engagements, being forced back to within half a mile of its camp, repaired thither about two o'clock and had a comfortable dinner. The Fifteenth suffered severely. The lieutenant-colonel and the major, the only field-officers with the regiment, wefe killed, two captains were killed and one wounded, one lieutenant was killed and six wounded. Colonel Veatch, with the Twenty-fifth Indiana and Fourteenth Illinois, continued fighting and manœuvring with skill and determination till the retreating division of Hurlbut passed along his rear. Colonel Veatch then reported to Hurlbut, and formed part of his line of defence in support of the reserve artillery at the close of the day.

PRENTISS AND W. H. L. WALLACE.

Prentiss' division in the front line, and W. H. L. Wallace's on the plateau between the river and Brier Creek, were more widely separated in camp than any other two divisions ; but in the contest of Sunday they operated together.

Colonel Moore, of the Twenty-first Missouri, being wounded early in the encounter with the Confederate advance, Lieutenant-Colonel Woodyard took command of the regiment, together with the accompanying detachment of the Twenty-fifth Missouri and four companies of the Sixteenth Wisconsin, sent out the night before to reinforce the pickets. Pushed by Shaver's brigade, he fell back after a struggle on the edge of a field to the farther side of a narrow ridge, about half a mile from camp, where he was joined by Colonel Peabody with the rest of the brigade. After a contest of half an hour, Shaver was repulsed and fell back. General A. S. Johnston observing men dropping out of the ranks of the retreating brigade, rallied it himself and ordered it to renew the attack. Peabody recoiled under the fresh onset, and, falling back, took his place, constituting the right of the line of battle of the division formed a quarter of a mile in advance of the camp.

Gladden's brigade, forming part of Bragg's corps, on the second line of Johnston's army, was moved forward to extend the right of Hardee on the first line, when, by the divergence of Lick Creek from Owl Creek, Hardee's line became inadequate to fill the distance between them. The line of Johnston's advance being oblique to the line of Prentiss' front, Gladden arrived in front of Prentiss' left after Shaver had become engaged with Peabody. Colonel Adams, who took command of the brigade upon the death of General Gladden, and who made the full report of the brigade, says they arrived in position at eight o'clock. Colonel Deas, who took command when Adams was wounded, says they arrived a little after seven. Colonel Loomis, who was in command on the return to Corinth, says in his report, made April 13th, that the engagement of this brigade began at half-past seven. Wheeling to the left and deploying into line, the brigade moved confidently forward. Gladden was mortally wounded and his command fell back in confusion. General Johnston ordered it to return to the attack, but, on inspecting its condition, countermanded the order.

Chalmers' brigade, coming up from the second line, made an impetuous charge. Jackson's brigade, which followed in rear of Chalmers, moved forward and joined in the attack. Prentiss fell back and made a stand immediately in front of his camp. After a gallant but short struggle, his division, about nine o'clock, gave way and fell back through his camp, leaving behind Powell's guns and caissons and two of Hickenlooper's guns, all the horses of Hickenlooper's two guns being killed. The line was broken and disordered by the tents. The Twenty-fifth Missouri, and portions of other regiments drifted to the rear. On the summit of a slope, covered by dense thicket, not far to the rear of his camp, Prentiss rallied the Eighteenth and Twenty-first Missouri, Twelfth Michigan, and Eighteenth Wisconsin. The Sixty-first Illinois and Sixteenth Wisconsin were also rallied, but detached to form in reserve to Hurlbut. The Twenty-third Missouri, arriving by boat at the landing after the battle had begun, moved out at once and took position in Prentiss' new line. In this position his left was near the extreme southern head of the ravine of Brier Creek; thence his line extended along an old, sunk, washed-out road running a little north of west, and reached nearly to the Corinth road. Prentiss in person put Hickenlooper's battery in position immediately to the right of the Corinth road, near the intersection of the roads. Prentiss' men used the road cut as a defence, lying down in it and firing from it. General Grant, visiting Prentiss, approved the position and directed him to hold it at all hazards. The order was obeyed. Continually assaulted by successive brigades, he repelled every attack and held the position till the close of the day.

General W. H. L. Wallace, commanding Smith's division, formed his regiments at eight o'clock. Some of the regiments loaded their wagons and received extra ammunition. At half-past eight o'clock the division moved ; McArthur with two of his regiments, the Ninth and Twelfth Illinois, went to support Stuart's brigade at its isolated camp at the extreme left of the National line, having sent the Thirteenth Missouri to Sherman, and left the Fourteenth Missouri and Eighty-first Ohio to guard the bridge over Snake Creek, on the Crump's Landing road. Wallace led his other two brigades to the support of Prentiss, placing Tuttle on Prentiss' right, and Sweeney to the right of Tuttle. Tuttle's left was about one hundred yards to the right of the Corinth road, and the division line extending northwestwardly behind a clear field, Sweeney's right reached the head of a wide, deep ravine—called in some of the Confederate reports a gorge—which ravine, filled with impenetrable thickets, extended from his right far to his rear and ran into the ravine of Brier Creek. Wallace added to the defence of this ravine by posting sharpshooters along its border. General Wallace detached the Eighth Iowa from Sweeney's brigade and placed it across the Corinth road, filling the interval between the two divisions.

Wallace's line was barely formed when, at ten o'clock, Gladden's brigade, now commanded by Colonel Adams, moved again against Prentiss. Advancing slowly up the slight ascent through impeding thickets, against an unseen foe, it encountered a blaze of fire from the summit, faltered, wavered, hesitated, retreated, and withdrew out of range. A. P. Stewart led his brigade against Wallace's front, was driven back, returned to the assault, and was again hurled back ; but still rallied, and moved once more in vain, to be again sent in retreat.

The Confederates gave this fatal slope the name "The Hornet's Nest." General Bragg ordered Gibson with his brigade to carry the position. The fresh column charged gallantly, but the deadly line of musketry in front, and an enfilading fire from the well-posted battery, mowed down his ranks ; and Gibson's brigade fell back discomfited. Gibson asked for artillery. None was at hand. Bragg ordered him to charge again. The colonels of the four regiments thought it hopeless. The order was given. The brigade struggled up the tangled ascent ; but once more met the inexorable fire that hurled them back. Four times Gibson charged, and was four times repulsed. Colonel Allen, of the Fourth Louisiana, one of Gibson's regiments, rode back to General Bragg to repeat the request for artillery. Stung by the answer, "Colonel Allen, I want no faltering now," he returned to his regiment, led it in a desperate dash up the slope, more persistent, and therefore more destructive, and returned with the fragment of his command that was not left strown upon the hill-side. As the line of Sherman and McClernand continually contracted as they fell back, the successive reinforcements pushed in toward the left of the Confederate line gradually pressed Hindman's two brigades—first wholly against McClernand's front, then against his left, then beyond his line. These two brigades were then moved to the front of W. H. L. Wallace. Flushed with victory, they advanced with confidence. The same resistless fire wounded Hindman and drove back his command. Led by General A. P. Stewart, the brigades gallantly advanced again and rushed against the fatal fire, only to be shivered into fragments that recoiled, to remain out of the contest for the rest of the day.

The commander of the Confederate Army was killed farther to the right, at half-past two o'clock in the afternoon. As the news of this loss spread, there was a feeling of uncertainty and visible relaxation of effort in parts of his command. In front of Prentiss and Wallace attack was suspended about an hour.

Hickenlooper's four guns, standing at the salient where Prentiss and Wallace joined, sweeping both fronts, had all day long been reaping bloody harvests among the lines of assailants that strove to approach. So near, yet so far ; in plain view, yet out of reach, the little battery exasperated the baffled brigades while it extorted their admiration. General Ruggles sent his staff officers in all directions to sweep in all the guns they could reach. He gives the names of eleven batteries and one section which he planted in a great crescent, pouring in a concentric fire. From this tornado of missiles Hickenlooper withdrew his battery complete, and, passing to the rear through Hurlbut's camp, reported to Sherman for further service.

The terrible fire of this artillery was supplemented by continued, but desultory infantry attacks. The Crescent regiment of Louisiana essayed to charge, but recoiled. Patton Anderson led his brigade up, but was driven back. About four o'clock, Hurlbut, whose right had joined Prentiss' left, finally gave way, and Bragg, following him, passed on to the rear of Prentiss. By half-past four the fighting in front of Sherman and McClernand had ceased, and Cheatham, Trabue, Johnson, and Russell, finding that Wallace could not be approached across the dense tangle filling the great ravine which protected his right, felt their way unopposed to the plateau in his rear, meeting the combined force under Bragg in front of Hurlbut's camp. General Polk collected in front of the steadfast men of Prentiss and Wallace all the

II.—7

other troops within reach, and at five o'clock, with one
mighty effort, surged against their line, now pounded by
Ruggles' batteries.

When Hurlbut fell back, leaving Prentiss and Wallace
entirely isolated, these two commanders consulted and resolved to hold their position at all hazards, and keep the
enemy from passing on to the landing. But when they became enveloped, almost encircled, the enemy having passed
behind them toward the landing and were closing upon the
Corinth road in their rear, Wallace ordered his command to
retire and cut a way through. Tuttle gave the order to his
brigade, which faced about to the rear and opened fire on
the forces closing behind. The Second and Seventh Iowa,
led by Colonel Tuttle, charged, cut their way through, and
marched to the landing. The Twelfth and Fourteenth Iowa,
lingering with the Eighth Iowa to cover the retreat of
Hickenlooper's battery, were too late, and found themselves
walled in. Colonel Baldwin, who had succeeded to the
command of the other brigade when Colonel Sweeney was
wounded, brought off part of his command; but two of his
regiments, the Fifty-eighth Illinois as well as the Eighth
Iowa, were securely enclosed. Wallace fell mortally wounded. Groups and squads of Prentiss' men succeeded in making their way out before the circle wholly closed. Prentiss,
with the remaining fragments of the two divisions, facing
the fire that surrounded them, made a desperate struggle. But further resistance was hopeless and was useless.
Prentiss, having never swerved from the position he was
ordered to hold, having lost everything but honor, surrendered the little band. According to his report, made after
his return from captivity, the number from both divisions
surrendered with him was 2,200. The statements vary as to
the precise hour of the surrender, and as to what command

surrendered last. Colonel Shaw, of the Fourteenth Iowa, who fought toward the rear before surrendering, says that at the time he yielded he compared watches with his captor, and both agreed it was about a quarter to six; he adds that the Eighth and Twelfth Iowa and Fifty-eighth Illinois surrendered at about the same time, and that the ground where they surrendered is about the spot marked by three black dots in the fork of the Purdy and the Lower Corinth roads, on Colonel George Thom's map of the field.

HURLBUT'S DIVISION.

It remains to describe the combat on the National left, where Hurlbut with two of his brigades, supporting Stuart's isolated brigade of Sherman's division and aided by two regiments of McArthur's brigade of W. H. L. Wallace's division, resisted a part of Bragg's corps and the reserves under General Breckenridge.

Colonel Stuart received word from Prentiss at half-past seven o'clock that the enemy was advancing in force. Shortly after, his pickets sent in word that the hostile column was in sight on the Bark road. He sent his adjutant, Loomis, to General Hurlbut for assistance, but Hurlbut was already in motion. Hurlbut, receiving notice from General Sherman, sent Veatch's brigade to his aid. Soon after, getting a request for support from Prentiss, he marched from his camp at twenty minutes after eight o'clock, with his first brigade commanded by Colonel Williams, of the Third Iowa, and his Third Brigade, commanded by Brigadier-General Lauman. Passing out by the Hamburg road, across the first small field and through a belt of timber beyond that, and into the large field that stretched to Stuart's camp, he formed the First Brigade in line near the southern side of the field, the Forty-first Illinois on the left, and the

Third Iowa on the right. The Third Brigade, Lauman's, the Seventeenth and Twenty-fifth Kentucky forming the left, and the Thirty-first and Forty-fourth Indiana the right, connected with Prentiss' left, and was posted like it, protected in front with dense thickets. General McArthur's two regiments appear to have operated on Stuart's right. The Sixteenth Wisconsin and Sixty-first Illinois, from Prentiss' division, formed in reserve in rear of the centre of Hurlbut's line.

Colonel Stuart, finding Mann's battery, supported by the Forty-first Illinois, coming to his aid and going into position by the headquarters of one of his regiments, the Seventy-first Ohio, formed his line, the Seventy-first Ohio and Fifty-fifth Illinois to the left of this battery and facing nearly west, the Fifty-fourth Ohio at their left and facing south. He sent four companies as skirmishers across the ravine to the south of his camp, which discharges eastwardly into Lick Creek. His skirmishers were unable to prevent the establishment of a hostile battery on the heights beyond the ravine. While he was on the bank of the ravine observing the enemy with his glass, Mann's battery, after firing a few rounds at the hostile battery at a range of eleven hundred yards, withdrew with the Forty-first Illinois back into the field, to connect with their brigade. The Seventy-first Ohio, without orders, at the same time retired. The Seventy-first Ohio was engaged in supporting distance of the brigade in its first combat, though without the knowledge of Colonel Stuart; but it was not with the brigade during the rest of the day. The adjutant, however, returned with a score of men after the regiment disappeared.

General Johnston, having personally seen the battle begun on his left and centre, proceeded to reconnoitre the National right and try the feasibility of turning it. Chalmers, called from his attack on Prentiss, retired a short distance and halted half an hour, waiting for a guide and further orders. He then marched directly south across the ravine which runs eastwardly and debouches into Lick Run near the site of Stuart's camp, and, advancing along the high land beyond, eastwardly toward the river, arrived opposite Stuart's camp. Here the fire of the skirmishers sent across the ravine by Stuart threw the Fifty-second Tennessee into disorder. Chalmers, finding it impossible to rally more than two companies of the regiment, ordered the remaining eight companies out of the line, and they took no further part in the battle.

Here Chalmers halted half an hour while Clanton's cavalry reconnoitered along the river. About ten o'clock, or a little later, Stuart having withdrawn his two remaining regiments, the Fifty-fourth Ohio and Fifth-fifth Illinois, back across the eastern extremity of the field to the summit of a short, abrupt ascent in timber, Chalmers deployed his brigade and advanced. The advantage of position partially compensated Stuart for his inferiority in numbers. A contest with musketry across the open field lasted some time without effect. Stuart reports it lasted two hours. Clanton moved his cavalry forward along the river bluffs toward Stuart's rear, around his left flank; Chalmers charged across the field, and Stuart retreated to another ridge in his rear, and again formed. Chalmers, being out of ammunition, and the wagons being far to the rear, halted till ammunition could be brought up.

Meanwhile, Jackson's brigade, the Third Brigade of Withers' division, marched to attack McArthur. The assault was gallantly made; but the troops, unable to stand the steady fire which they encountered, fell back. Being rallied after a rest, they renewed the attack. For a long time the fate of the obstinate struggle was undecided. At length

McArthur's two regiments, pounded by well-posted batteries, yielded to Jackson's persistent attack, after the Ninth Illinois had lost 61 killed and 287 wounded, and withdrew, steadily and in order, to a new position.

Withers' First Brigade—Gladden's having been disordered in its first attack on Prentiss, when General Gladden was killed—remained an hour at halt in Prentiss' camp. After its sharp repulse in the later attack, the brigade drifted to its right, following the course of preceding brigades, came in front of Hurlbut's line, and moved to the attack. Lauman's brigade, of Hurlbut's division, had remained undisturbed for an hour after taking position. A skirmish line which he had posted in front reported an advance of the enemy. Artillery from a distance in front opened fire. At the first shot which fell in the Thirteenth Ohio Battery, posted in the field to Lauman's left, with the right of Williams' brigade, the entire battery deserted their guns and fled. Shortly after the battle the men were, by order, distributed among other batteries; the Thirteenth was blotted out, and on Ohio's roster its place remained a blank throughout the war.

Soon, a line of gleaming steel was seen above the dense undergrowth in Lauman's front. It advanced steadily till about one hundred yards from his line. A sheet of fire blazed from the front of the brigade. The men, restrained till then, fired rapidly but coolly. The fire could not be resisted or endured. Gladden's brigade, now commanded by Colonel Adams, was arrested in its march, broken, and fell back. Three times the brigade rallied and returned to the assault. Once, a portion advanced to within a few paces of the Thirty-first Indiana. But every charge was vain, and Colonel Adams, the commander, being wounded, the brigade, discomfited, withdrew.

After the termination of this engagement, several regiments—either the Gladden brigade, now commanded by Colonel Deas, or one of the brigades of Breckenridge's reserve—moved into the field to the left of Lauman. Colonel Williams, commanding Hurlbut's first brigade, had been killed in an artillery duel across the field, and the brigade, now commanded by Colonel Pugh, had been drawn back from the field, behind a fence along its northern boundary. The force that moved into the field was not only confronted by the brigade under Colonel Pugh, but its flank was commanded by the Seventeenth and Twenty-fifth Kentucky, which General Lauman promptly wheeled to the left, against the fence bounding the westerly face of the field. The assault made in this field was gallant and deliberate, but brief and sanguinary. Pugh's command remained still until the lines, advancing over the open field, were near. Then rising, they poured in a volley, and continued firing into the smoke until no bullets were heard whistling back from the front. The two Kentucky regiments poured in their fire upon the flank, and when the smoke cleared away, the field was so thickly strewn with bodies, that the Third Iowa, supposing it was the hostile force lying down, began to reopen fire upon them.

Before Withers' division became thus engaged with Hurlbut, McArthur, and Stuart, General Johnston had dispatched Trabue's brigade, of Breckenridge's reserve, off to his extreme left, to report to General Beauregard, who, stationed at Shiloh Church, was superintending operations in that quarter. The three brigades, Bowen, Statham, Trabue, composing the reserve, had marched in rear of General Johnston's right in echelon, at intervals of eight hundred yards. Johnston, observing with anxiety the stubborn resistance opposed to Withers' division, and eager to crush the National right, called up the remaining brigades of the reserve, Bowen and Statham, and pushed them forward. Bowen was first engaged, and the National left, in a series of encounters with the increased force in its front, gradually but slowly receded, always forming and rallying on the next ridge in rear of the one abandoned.

The Forty-first Illinois, constituting the left of Hurlbut's division, held its position, and the Thirty-second Illinois was moved from its place to support the Forty-first. The afternoon was come. Johnston directed Statham's brigade against this position. Statham deployed under cover of a ridge, facing and commanded by the higher ridge held by the Illinois regiments, and marched in line up the slope. On reaching the summit, coming into view and range, he was received by a fire that broke his command, and his regiments fell back behind the slope in confusion. Battle's Tennessee regiment on the right alone maintained its position and advanced. Lytle's Tennessee regiment three times rallied and advanced; but, unable to stand the fire, fell back. Every time it fell back, the Thirty-second Illinois threw an oblique fire into Battle's regiment, aiding the direct fire of the Forty-first, and preventing Battle's further advance. The Forty-fifth Tennessee could not be urged up the slope. Squads would leave the ranks, run up to a fence, fire, and fall back to place; but the regiment would not advance. General Breckenridge, foiled and irritated, rode to General Johnston and complained he had a Tennessee regiment that would not fight. Governor Harris, of Tennessee, who was with Johnston, remonstrated, and riding to the Forty-fifth, appealed to it, but in vain. General Johnston moved to the front of the brigade, now standing in line, rode slowly along the front, promised to lead them himself, and appealed to them to follow. The halting soldiers were roused to enthusiasm. Johnston, Breckenridge, and Governor Harris in front, followed by the brigade, charged up the slope and down the hollow beyond. Unchecked by the hot fire of the Illinois regiments, they pushed up the higher slope, and the position was gained.

The Illinois regiments fell back slowly, halting at intervals to turn and fire, and were not pursued. One of those Parthian shots struck General Johnston, cut an artery, and, no surgeon being at hand, he bled to death in a few minutes. His body was carried at once by his staff back to Corinth. General Beauregard, at his station at Shiloh Church, was notified of the death, and assumed command. Albert Sydney Johnston was a man of pure life, and, like McPherson, full of the traits that call out genuine and devoted friendships. He was esteemed by many the ablest general in the Confederate service. His death was deplored in the South as a fatal loss. It was half-past two when Johnston fell. The loss paralyzed operations in that part of the field, and for an hour there was here a lull. The two Illinois regiments, though not followed, failed to rally, and fell back to a bluff near the landing, where Colonel Webster was putting batteries into position.

General Bragg, hearing of the death of General Johnston while he was superintending operations in front of Prentiss and W. H. L. Wallace, rode to the Confederate right. He there found a strong force, consisting of three parts, without a common head : General Breckenridge, with two brigades of his reserve division, pressing forward; General Withers, with his division greatly exhausted and taking a temporary rest ; and General Cheatham, with his division of Polk's corps, to their left and rear. Bragg at once assumed command, and began to assemble these divisions and form them for a general advance. Hurlbut, observing these preparations, moved Lauman's brigade, which had already twice replenished its boxes and expended one hundred rounds of cartridges—to his left to fill the gap made by the retreat of the Thirty-second and Forty-first Illinois. Willard's battery, that accompanied McArthur's brigade, was posted near the road from the landing to Hamburg. Hurlbut brought up two twenty-pound guns of Major Cavender's artillery, which were served by Surgeon Cornine and Lieutenant Edwards. A little after four, according to Bragg, about half-past three according to Hurlbut, Bragg moved forward. The artillery, aided by the rapid fire of Hurlbut's infantry, checked the first impulse and made the advancing line pause. Hurlbut, taking advantage of the lull, and first notifying Prentiss, withdrew Lauman's brigade and the artillery. Bragg's line advanced again. Hurlbut attempted to make another stand in front of his camp, but the attempt was ineffectual. He fell back to the height behind Webster's batteries.

The Third Iowa and Twenty-eighth Illinois, under Colonel Pugh, made a desperate effort to maintain their position, but were ordered by General Hurlbut to fall back when Lauman retired. These two regiments fell back fighting, forming wherever the ground gave vantage, and turning upon their pursuers. In the little field they halted and replenished their cartridge-boxes. Here the Twenty-second Alabama attacked them, but was so roughly handled that it took no further part in the contest that day. As these two regiments fell back thus slowly, from time to time turning at bay, portions of Bragg's command were pushing behind them and the troops of Hardee, coming from the front of Sherman and McClernand, were reaching toward their front. A narrow gap was left, and through a gauntlet of fire, still fighting, the little band pressed on and joined Hurlbut behind Webster's artillery.

The gunboat Tyler, commanded by Lieutenant Gwin, fired from ten minutes to three o'clock until ten minutes to four upon Breckenridge's brigades, and, joined by the Lexington, commanded by Lieutenant Shirk, fired later upon the portion of Bragg's command close to the river-bank, for thirty-five minutes. This fire drove a battery from its position, threw Gibson's brigade and a portion of Trabue's brigade into disorder, killed ten and wounded many of Wood's brigade, killed and wounded a number of Anderson's brigade, and compelled it to seek shelter in a ravine.

As the National lines were drifting back toward the landing, Colonel Webster, of General Grant's staff, gathered all the artillery within reach—Major Cavender's six twenty-pounders, Silversparre's twenty-pound Parrotts, and some light batteries—on a commanding position from a quarter to half a mile from the landing. Immediately above the landing a wide and deep ravine opens to the river. For some distance back from the river its bottom was filled with backwater and was impassable. Half a mile back it was still deep, abrupt, and wet, though passable for infantry. Here Colonel Webster gathered from thirty-five to fifty guns. Two of Hurlbut's batteries—Mann's, commanded by Lieutenant Brotzman, and Ross'—had done brilliant service; Brotzman's battery of four pieces had fired off one hundred and ninety-four rounds per gun. Ross' battery was lost in the retreat. Brotzman lost so many horses that he was able to bring off only three guns. These took place in Webster's frowning line. Hurlbut was joined at this position by half of Veatch's brigade, which had been with McClernand through the day, and reformed his division in support of the artillery. General Grant directed him to assume command of all regiments and coherent fragments near. The Forty-eighth Ohio, of Buckland's brigade, being then at the landing, some of W. H.

L. Wallace's regiments, that succeeded in breaking through the encircling force, and other detachments, reported to him. Squads of men, separated from their commands, fell in. Hurlbut thus gathered in support of the artillery a force in line which he estimated at four thousand men.

General Bragg proposed to push his success and attempted to withdraw his two divisions, Ruggles' and Withers', from the tumult which accompanied the surrender, and ordered them to press forward and assault the position to which Hurlbut had fallen back. When Ruggles received Bragg's order for farther advance, one of his brigades, Pond's, was on the extreme Confederate left, near Owl Creek; Gibson's brigade was in confusion, caused by the fire of the gunboats; Anderson's was apart in a ravine, taking shelter from the same fire. But Ruggles began at once to assemble what force he could. Of Withers' division, the First Brigade was scattered. The brigades of Jackson and Chalmers received the order while they were resting in the field where the Third Iowa had rested and filled their cartridge-boxes, and where Jackson was about to replenish the empty boxes of his men. Withers immediately moved these two brigades forward to the deep ravine whose farther bank was crowned with the grim line of artillery, behind and to the right of which stood Hurlbut's command.

While there was this activity at the front, the aspect at the rear, about Shiloh Church, where General Beauregard kept his position, was very different. As the Confederate lines advanced, men dropping out of the ranks filled the woods with a penumbra of stragglers. Hunger and fatigue, stimulated by the remembrance of abandoned camps passed through, later in the day led squads—Beauregard and some of his staff say, led regiments—to straggle back from the fighting front to the restful and attractive rear. Language cannot be stronger than that used by General Beauregard. The fire of the gunboats, many of the shells passing over the high river-bank and exploding far inland, appeared even more formidable than it really was; and Beauregard was assured by a despatch, which he received that day on the field, that Buell, instead of being near Pittsburg, was, in fact, before Florence, and could not effect a junction. It must have been about five o'clock or a little later when Beauregard sent an order to his command to retire and go into bivouac. The order was delivered by his staff not only to corps commanders, but directly to commanders of divisions and brigades. General Ruggles, while attempting to assemble a force in pursuance of Bragg's order, received the command to retire.

According to Withers' report, he moved his division forward and just entered a steep and precipitous ravine when he was met by a terrific fire. He sent to the rear for reinforcements and ordered his brigade commanders to charge the batteries in front. The orders were about being obeyed, when, to his astonishment, he observed a large portion of his command move rapidly by the left flank away from under the fire. He then learned that this was in accordance with General Beauregard's orders, delivered directly to the brigade commanders. Jackson reports that he began a charge, but his men, being without ammunition, could not be urged up the height in face of the fire of Hurlbut and the batteries. Leaving his men lying down, he rode to the rear to get an order to withdraw, when he met a staff officer bearing such an order from General Beauregard. General Chalmers plunged into the ravine, and the order to retire did not reach him. He was not aware that his brigade alone, of all the Confederate Army, was continuing the battle. He brought Gage's battery up to his aid, but this battery was soon

knocked to pieces by the fire of the heavier National artillery. The gunboats, having previously taken position opposite the mouth of the ravine, opened fire as soon as the assault began. They opened fire at thirty-five minutes past
five.

Chalmers had not ended his useless attempt when the
boats bearing Ammen's brigade of Nelson's division of
Buell's army crossed the river and landed. General Nelson, when ordered by General Grant, early in the morning,
to move up the river, sent out a party to discover a route. No
practicable way was found near the river ; one, a little inland, was ascertained, practicable for infantry, but not for
wheels. The division moved at one o'clock. General Ammen's brigade, composed of the Thirty-sixth Indiana and
the Sixth and Twenty-fourth Ohio, being in advance, crossed
the river first. The Thirty-sixth Indiana, landing first,
pushed up the bluff through a great mob of fugitives from
the field, some thousands in number, and, by direction of
General Grant, General Ammen sent it forward to the support of the batteries. One soldier was killed while the regiment was forming ; one was killed and one wounded after
it reached its position. The Sixth Ohio marched up under
like order in reserve to the Thirty-sixth Indiana. The
Twenty-fourth Ohio marched half a mile to the right of the
batteries, scoured the country half a mile out to the front
without finding any enemy, and there went into bivouac.
The day's battle was over.

Prentiss was driven back through his camp about nine
o'clock ; Sherman was forced from his about ten o'clock ;
at the same time, Stuart took position in rear of his.
McClernand was compelled finally to abandon his camp
about half-past two, and at half-past four Hurlbut fell back
through his. When night came, the National troops held

W. H. L. Wallace's camp and an adjoining portion of Hurlbut's, while Beauregard's army occupied Sherman's, McClernand's, and Prentiss'.

When Prentiss and Sherman were attacked, there was a
wide gap between their lines. A little after ten o'clock the
National line was connected, Sherman on the right, McClernand next, then W. H. L. Wallace, and next, on his left,
Prentiss, and Hurlbut and McArthur filling the space between Prentiss and Stuart. The right was gradually forced
back on a curve till, at half-past four o'clock, there was a gap
between McClernand and Wallace. Hurlbut held his ground
till four o'clock, but by half-past four he retreated, leaving
Prentiss' left in air. Through the two gaps thus made the
Confederate left and right poured in and encircled Prentiss
and Wallace. After their surrender there was no fighting,
except Chalmers' bold, but idle assault.

In this day's battle the National loss was nearly ten thousand killed, wounded, and captured. The Confederate loss
was as great in killed and wounded, but the loss in prisoners
was small.

CHAPTER VII.

SHILOH—NIGHT, AND MONDAY.

THE vice of the formation of Johnston's army into three long, thin, parallel lines, together with the broken character of the ground and the variable obstinacy of resistance encountered, produced a complete and inextricable commingling of commands. General Beauregard left it to the discretion of the different commanders to select the place for bivouac for the night.

Colonel Pond, retiring from his disastrous repulse toward the close of the afternoon, found himself wholly separated by an interval of more than a quarter of a mile from the nearest support, the whole of the Confederate left having drifted from him toward the south-east. Assembling all his brigade, except the Crescent Regiment, which had become detached, and recalling his battery—Ketchum's—he remembered that the special duty had been assigned to him, by General Bragg, of guarding the flank along Owl Creek. When night fell, he moved to his rear and then to his left, and bivouacked in line facing to the east, on the high land west of Brier Creek. Ketchum's battery was placed in a field a little back from the ravine. He posted pickets to his rear as well as to his front. The other two brigades of Ruggles' division spent the night to the east of Shiloh Church.

Jackson's brigade, of Withers' division, when it recoiled

from its fatal attack on Hurlbut and the reserve artillery, went to pieces. Jackson with the battery marched to Shiloh Church and reported to General Beauregard. He saw nothing more of his brigade till he rejoined it at Corinth. Chalmers, abandoning his vain assault, was astonished to find that the army had fallen back, leaving him alone. He fell back to the field where Prentiss surrendered, and there rested. Of the remaining brigade, Gladden's, the merest fragment cohered; this little band, or detachment, bivouacked near the Hamburg road. Trabue's brigade, except one regiment which had become separated, spent the night in the tents of McDowell's brigade camp; Breckenridge's other two brigades were between Shiloh Church and the river.

Of General Polk's command, Clark's division, though partially scattered, rested, the greater portion of it, between Breckenridge and Shiloh Church. The other division, Cheatham's, which remained the freshest and least disordered command in Beauregard's army, moved off the field; and, accompanied by General Polk and one regiment of Clark's division, marched back to its camp of Saturday night.

Of Hardee's corps, so much of Cleburne's brigade as remained with him, slept in Prentiss' camp; Wood's brigade slept in McClernand's camp; Shaver's brigade was disintegrated and dissipated.

In the National army, what men were left of Prentiss' division were gathered about the landing and with Hurlbut. The regiments of W. H. L. Wallace that had escaped capture returned to their division camp. Hurlbut after dark moved his division out to the front of the reserve artillery. Being relieved by General Nelson, he formed his line with its left near the reserve artillery and the right near McClernand. McClernand's command bivouacked along the

11

eastern face of the camp-ground of W. H. L. Wallace's division. Sherman's left joined McClernand; his right, Buckland's brigade, lay along the field at the south flank of McArthur's brigade camp, and along the east bank of the ravine of Brier Creek. Stuart's brigade, the Fortieth Illinois of McDowell's brigade, and the Forty-eighth Ohio of Buckland's brigade spent the night near the reserve artillery.

Captain Baxter, of General Grant's staff, brought to Lewis Wallace at eleven or half-past eleven, a verbal order to move his division. The First Brigade had already moved out to Stony Lonesome, and the division was ready to march. General Wallace believed the attack at Pittsburg was a feint, and that the real attack was to be made at Crump's Landing, on account of the great accumulation of stores at that point, and desired the order requiring him to move away from Crump's Landing should be in writing. Captain Baxter wrote and gave him an order to march to the Purdy road, form there on Sherman's right, and then act as circumstances should require. The two brigades at Stony Lonesome were at once put in motion. When the head of the division had just reached Snake Creek, not much more than a mile in an air-line from the right of Sherman's camp, Captain Rowley came up and informed Wallace of the state of affairs, and that the National line had fallen back. Wallace countermarched the two brigades to keep his right in front, retraced his steps (being joined on the way by Major Rawlins, Grant's adjutant, and by Colonel McPherson) the greater part of the way to Stony Lonesome, and there took a rude cross-road which came into the river road from Crump's to Pittsburg Landing, about a mile from the bridge which had been guarded for his approach. McPherson and Rawlins confirmed Captain Rowley's statement of the disastrous falling back of the National lines toward the river.

The wagons were not allowed to accompany the column, but continued on through Stony Lonesome to Crump's Landing, and the Fifty-sixth Ohio, and one gun from Thurber's battery were detached to guard them. Whittlesey's brigade, at Adamsville, received at two o'clock the order to march. Sending the wagons with the Sixty-eighth Ohio as guard to Crump's Landing, the remaining three regiments pushed through the mud, the field officers dismounting to let broken-down men ride, and overtook the other brigades as they were beginning to cross Snake Creek. The Twenty-fourth Indiana in advance, crossing the bridge just after sunset, deployed skirmishers in front, marched along the road along the east bank of Brier Creek, and halted in front of the camp of the Fourteenth Missouri, which regiment was occupying its camp. The Twentieth Ohio, the rear regiment of the division, halted on the bank of Brier Creek ravine, in front of the camp of the Eighty-first Ohio, at eight o'clock. The division facing to the right, making a front to the west, along the ravine, brought the Twenty-fourth Indiana to the left and the Twentieth Ohio to the right of the division. The batteries having been left at the junction of the cross-road and the river road, till all the infantry had crossed, followed in their rear, and were posted near the bank.

The remainder of Nelson's division followed Ammen's brigade late in the evening. Crittenden's division arrived in the night. McCook receiving orders to hasten forward in the morning, while twelve miles out from Savannah, halted at the outskirts of the village at seven o'clock P.M., rested his men two hours, marched to the landing, seized such boats as were there and such as arrived, and reached Pittsburg Landing at five o'clock Monday morning with Rousseau's brigade and one regiment of Kirk's brigade.

General Grant and General Buell met at Sherman's headquarters in the evening; it was there agreed that Buell
with his army should in the morning attack on the left, and
Grant's immediate command should attack on the right.
Buell formed Nelson's division about two hundred yards
in front of the reserve artillery, with his left near the river,
facing south. Crittenden, when he arrived, was placed in
rear of Nelson, half a mile from the landing, where his command stood at arms all night. At eleven o'clock a heavy
rain began to pour. All the National troops and most of the
Confederate lay on the ground without shelter. The gunboats every fifteen minutes through the night fired a shell
over the woods, to explode far inland and banish sleep.

Early Monday morning, Nelson on the extreme left, on
the Hamburg road, and Lewis Wallace on the extreme right,
by Snake Creek, moved to the attack. Beauregard knew
then that Buell had arrived and the junction of the two National armies had been effected. The opening of the battle
proclaimed what the conclusion would be.

Nelson moved in line with Ammen's brigade on the left,
Bruce's in the centre, and Hazen's on the right, his left extending a little beyond the Hamburg road towards the river.
A remnant of Gladden's brigade, between two and three
hundred men, under Colonel Deas, some fragments of some
of the regiments of Jackson's brigade, with some regiments
that had strayed from their proper commands, the Fourth
Kentucky from Trabue's brigade, the First Tennessee from
Stephens' brigade, the One Hundred and Fifty-fourth Tennessee from General B. R. Johnson's brigade, and the Crescent
Regiment from Pond's brigade, scattered about, were roused
by Nelson's advance and retired before it. At six o'clock
Nelson was halted by Buell to allow Crittenden's division to
complete its deployment and form on Nelson's right. Nelson

again advanced. General Withers meanwhile had thrown the heterogeneous fragments into an organized force, added Chalmers' brigade to it, and strengthened it by the addition of three batteries. Nelson, when he again advanced, came upon this consolidated line, which drove him back. Nelson was without artillery. His batteries, unable to get through the soft mud which the infantry traversed, remained behind at Savannah. General Buell sent to his aid Mendenhall's battery from Crittenden's division. The rapid and accurate fire of Mendenhall's guns silenced the central opposing battery. Hazen's brigade charged upon it, captured the guns and drove in retreat the cannoneers and their support. Bowen's brigade of Breckenridge's reserve corps, commanded by Colonel Martin since General Bowen was wounded Sunday afternoon, was coming up in support. Colonel Martin made his brigade lie down in a ravine till the torrent of fugitives passed over, then rising, charged the pursuers. Hazen's brigade, torn by the fire of two batteries, one on each flank, and now charged by a fresh brigade, suffered in a short time more than half the whole loss suffered by the division in the entire day. The loss of the division in killed and wounded, was 90 killed and 558 wounded. The Forty-first Ohio, in Hazen's brigade, out of a total engaged of 371, lost 140 killed and wounded. The shattered regiments streamed back in confusion, leaving a gap in the division line

Ammen's brigade was sorely pressed. Constituting the left of the army, it was in constant risk of being turned. Bruce's brigade, now put in hazard by the recession of Hazen, could give only indirect assistance to Ammen. Just then, Terrill's regular battery, of four twelve-pounders (Napoleons) and two ten-pound Parrotts, having arrived from Savannah, and missed its way to McCook's division, was ordered by General Buell to Nelson's relief. Dashing out to the skirmish line in front of Colonel Ammen, in order to get the range of the enemy's batteries, Terrill's guns became the target of the concentrated fire of the opposing batteries and the line of infantry. He was compelled to retire ; but, firing as he retired, he kept at a distance the long line that followed and essayed to charge. Colonel Tuttle, who had been marching what was left of W. H. L. Wallace's division in reserve, in rear of Nelson and Crittenden, sent the Second Iowa forward in aid of Terrill. At the same time the Fortieth Illinois, of McDowell's brigade, Sherman's division, which had been marching in reserve to Nelson, filed to the front around Ammen's left flank, and the Confederate line retired to their position in the timber. Ammen's line, which fell back under the galling fire called out by Terrill's artillery charge, now returned to the front and occupied the timber where the enemy had been. It was now nearly two o'clock. There was no more fighting in Nelson's front. Terrill's battery suffered so severely that the Sixth Ohio was detailed as its special support, and supplied artillerists from its ranks. From an advanced position in Nelson's front, upon his skirmish line, this battery succeeded in opening an enfilading fire upon the troops in front of McCook, and one section advanced far enough to take in reverse the batteries that were engaged with Crittenden and McCook.

General Crittenden's division moved a little after five o'clock to Nelson's right. Colonel W. S. Smith's brigade connected with Nelson and continued his line. General J. T. Boyle's brigade was formed in rear of the left wing of Smith's brigade. A little after six o'clock McCook marched to the front with Rousseau's brigade, and formed on Crittenden's right, but facing to the west. The Fourteenth Wisconsin, assigned to Prentiss' division, not arriving at Pittsburg till Monday morning, reported to General Crittenden, and acted during the day as a part of Colonel Smith's brigade. General Buell describes the line thus formed as follows : "The force under my command occupied a line of about a mile and a half. In front of Nelson's division was an open field, partially screened toward his right by a skirt of woods, which extended beyond the enemy's line, with a thick undergrowth in front of the left brigade of Crittenden's division ; then an open field in front of Crittenden's right and McCook's left, and in front of McCook's right woods again, with a dense undergrowth. The ground, nearly level in front of Nelson, formed a hollow in front of Crittenden, and fell into a small creek or ravine, which empties into Owl Creek, in front of McCook. What I afterward learned was the Hamburg road (which crosses Lick Creek a mile from its mouth) passed perpendicularly through the line of battle near Nelson's left. A short distance in rear of the enemy's left, on high, open ground, were the encampments of McClernand's and Sherman's divisions, which the enemy held." This line is almost identical with the line held by McArthur, Hurlbut, Prentiss, and Wallace, Sunday afternoon. Buell's cavalry was not brought up, and, from want of transportation, only three batteries—Bartlett's and Mendenhall's of Crittenden's division, and Terrill's of McCook's division. But these were served with remarkable efficiency.

When Crittenden took position, his skirmishers were advanced across the open field to the edge of the timber in front. · This dense growth, called in the reports "chapparal" and "jungle," covered both slopes of a hollow, which was threaded by a rivulet with muddy borders, and was the scene of many a bloody repulse the day before, in the repeated assaults upon Prentiss. The skirmishers soon became engaged, and a battery concealed in woods on rising ground be-

yond, played upon the troops in line. The skirmishers retired
to the line, but were sent back to their originial position,
while Bartlett's battery silenced the hostile battery, and, by
accurate fire, compelled it several times to shift its position.
A line of battle appearing in the timber preparing to charge,
the skirmishers were called back, Bartlett swept the bushes
with canister and shrapnell, Boyle's brigade charged into
the brush, encountered the fire of the Confederate line at
close quarters, replied, charged, and drove the enemy through
the timber to an open field beyond. The enemy rapidly
crossed the field and took position in woods on its farther
side. A line of cavalry appearing at one end of the field,
which was also commanded by the enemy's battery, Boyle
withdrew his regiments to their original position. Bartlett's
battery, aided by Mendenhall's, was in constant activity.
The infantry, with intervening pauses of cessation, met and
made charges into the chapparal. Mendenhall's battery, in
the course of the day, expended five hundred and twenty-six
rounds of ammunition, or about eighty-eight to the gun.
Bartlett, by noon, had fired his entire supply, six hundred
rounds, and took his battery to the landing to replenish.
When he returned, the fighting had ceased. After an hour
of quiet, a furious attack was made on Smith's brigade. The
contest that ensued is described in Colonel Smith's report:
"The enemy soon yielded, when a running fight commenced,
which extended about a mile to our front, where we captured
a battery and shot the horses and many of the cannoneers.
Owing to the obstructed nature of the ground, the enthusias-
tic courage of the majority of our men, the laggard discharge
of their duty by many, and the disgraceful cowardice of
some, our line had been transformed into a column of attack,
representing the various grades of courage, from reckless
daring to ignominious fear. At the head of this column stood

a few heroic men, not adequately supported, when the enemy returned to the attack with three fresh regiments in good order. We were driven back by these nearly to the first position occupied by our line, when we again rallied and moved forward toward the battery. Reaching a ravine to the right, and about six hundred paces from the battery, we halted and awaited the assistance of Mendenhall's battery, which was brought into action on a knoll within half a mile of the enemy's battery, which it immediately silenced. We then advanced and captured it the second time, and succeeded in holding it despite the efforts of the enemy to repulse us." This charge entirely shattered Cleburne's brigade, and it disappeared from the contest. This ended the battle in Crittenden's front, and Mendenhall's battery advanced and fired on the flank of the column, by that time retiring before McCook's division. The force which General Crittenden engaged was commanded by General Breckenridge, and consisted of one of Breckenridge's brigades—Statham's—aided by the brigades of Russell and A. P. Stewart, from Polk's corps. These two brigades constituted Clark's division, but General Clark having been wounded the previous day, the brigades were under Breckenridge's immediate command. To these was added Cleburne's brigade, reduced to one-third of its numbers. One-third was killed and wounded before Buckland's brigade, Sunday morning; one-third had straggled to the rear; the remaining third rallied to enter into Monday's battle.

In accordance with the direction of General Buell, McCook deployed Rousseau's brigade into line facing toward Shiloh Church. The Fifteenth Michigan, intended for Prentiss' division, being now without assignment, reported to McCook, and was by him attached for the day to Rousseau's brigade. General Beauregard still held his own position near the

II.—8

church, and as the line of inevitable retreat was by the road
passing by the church, it was necessary that his force should
hold this position to the last. It was a centre to which
stragglers and fragments of commands had drifted during
the night. Monday morning the greater part of Beauregard's army reported there, and, though much was despatched
thence to other quarters, portions so despatched returned
to take part in the final conflict. Pond's brigade, after its
rapid retreat from Lewis Wallace's front, had a fatiguing
march before finally settling into position. He says in his
report: "I was ordered by General Ruggles to form on the
extreme left and rest my left on Owl Creek. While proceeding to execute this order, I was ordered to move by the
rear of the main line to support the extreme right of General
Hardee's line. Having taken my position to support General Hardee's right, I was again ordered by General Beauregard to advance and occupy the crest of a ridge in the edge
of an old field. My line was just formed in this position
when General Polk ordered me forward to support his line.
While moving to the support of General Polk, an order
reached me from General Beauregard to report to him with
my command at his headquarters." Ruggles' division and
Cheatham's division, with one regiment of Clark's, were put
on the Confederate left of Shiloh Church; Wood's brigade
and Trabue's brigade to the right. Russell and A. P. Stewart were first sent to oppose Crittenden, but were afterward
shifted toward the Confederate left, to McCook's front.
The report of Colonel Thompson, Beauregard's aid-de-camp,
to General Beauregard, states: "About 11.30 o'clock it was
apparent that the enemy's main attack was on our left, and
our forces began to yield to the vigor of his attack."

When Rousseau's brigade was formed, his right was in
the air. McCook held it in place till Kirk's brigade arrived

from Savannah, and occupied the time exploring the ground to his front and right. Kirk having arrived, McCook moved Rousseau's brigade across a ravine to a rising ground a few hundred yards in advance, and placed Kirk's brigade in reserve of Rousseau's right, to protect the exposed flank. A company of regulars (there were three battalions of regulars in Rousseau's command) was sent into the woods as skirmishers. In less than an hour the skirmishers were driven back and followed by the Fourth Kentucky Regiment and Fourth Alabama Battalion belonging to Trabue's brigade. After a fierce attack for twenty minutes, the assailants fell back before the rapid and well-directed fire of Rousseau's men and retired out of sight in the timber. Trabue's regiments rallied and quickly returned to the assault with greater vigor than before. The steady fire of Rousseau's men again drove them to retreat ; Rosseau advanced into the timber, passed through it to an open field, when Trabue, who, with three regiments was engaged with McClernand, united the two portions of his brigade and charged furiously upon Rousseau. After a desperate struggle Trabue gave way ; Rousseau captured two guns and repossessed McClernand's headquarters.

This advance drew Rousseau away from Crittenden, while it connected him with McClernand ; exposed his left, while it covered his right. Colonel Willich, who had arrived with the Thirty-second Indiana, passed around to the left, and, with regiment in column doubled on the centre, charged upon the enemy in that quarter, drove him into the timber, then deploying in line opened fire. Willich became subject to so hot a fire—mainly, he reports, from the National troops —that he was compelled to retire. Dressing his lines he charged again. Observing undue excitement in his men, he halted the regiment, and in the midst of the battle exercised the men in the manual of arms. Having thus steadied them, he resumed the charge and again drove the enemy into the timber. Rousseau's command having exhausted their cartridges, Kirk's brigade took place in the line, while Rousseau, behind them, replenished from the supply which General McCook had already procured. Gibson's brigade having now arrived, was deployed, about two o'clock, on the left. The two armies were concentrating about Shiloh Church. Gibson's left flank being twice threatened and partially turned, the Forty-ninth Ohio twice, under fire, changed front to the rear on the right company with precision. Veatch's brigade, of Hurlbut's division, which had been acting in reserve, was moved forward by McCook and extended his left. The division being now sorely pressed by the enemy's artillery, Major Taylor, Sherman's chief of artillery, brought forward Bouton's battery and assigned part to each brigade. The section assigned to Gibson quickly silenced the batteries in his front. McCook was now connected with the forces to his right.

McClernand's command consisted—Monday morning—of the Forty-sixth Illinois, of Hurlbut's division, constituting his right; the Twentieth, Seventeenth, Forty-third, Forty-fifth, Forty-eighth, and Forty-ninth Illinois, of his own division, being his First and Second Brigades, and, on his left, the Fifty-third Ohio, of Sherman's division, and the Eighty-first Ohio, of W. H. L. Wallace's division. Except the two flanking regiments, the Forty-sixth Illinois and the Eighty-first Ohio, the regiments were extremely reduced. After firing had opened by Nelson and by Lewis Wallace, McClernand moved across the ravine of Brier Creek to the large open field, where his line was dressed; McAllister's battery was brought up and engaged a battery posted beyond, or in the proper front of, McClernand's First Brigade camp. Lewis Wallace's batteries beyond the timber to the northwest,

and a battery with Sherman in the same direction, joined in
the artillery combat. The Confederate battery becoming
silent, McClernand moved forward and entered the camp of
his First Brigade, being the northwestern extremity of his
camp, without having encountered opposing infantry. It was
discovered that a body of the enemy was advancing beyond
the left of the line. McClernand moved by the flank to the
left till the left regiments came to a field in rear of his camp,
and charged across it against a battery and its supports on the
farther side. The Fifty-third and Eighty-first Ohio recoiled,
were ordered back, fell to the rear in some disorder, and the
whole line retired. The Twenty-eighth Illinois was moved
forward from Hurlbut's reserve and added to McClernand's
left. The line again advanced, pushed the enemy back
through McClernand's camp, where he made a stand, and
McClernand was again compelled to yield. General McCook
now extended his right by throwing forward the Louisville
Legion. The two divisions connected, and the Twenty-
eighth Illinois returned to the reserve

Sherman, being ordered by General Grant early in the
morning to advance and recapture his camps, sent his staff
out to gather in the members of his command. Colonel Sul-
livan marched the Forty-eighth Ohio, at dawn, out from the
reserve artillery, and Buckland's brigade was complete.
Colonel Stuart was found near the landing with two regiments of his brigade, and a small detachment of the Third,
the Seventy-first Ohio. The Thirteenth Missouri, temporarily attached to Sherman, which had become entangled
with McClernand's command the previous afternoon, and
bivouacked at night in his line, was regained. Portions
of the Fifty-seventh and Seventy-seventh Ohio still adhered.
Major Taylor, chief of artillery, brought Lieutenant Wood's
battery. The column being formed, he marched by the

flank toward the west to the bluffs of Owl Creek, and along them to an open field at the extreme right of McClernand's camp, and awaited the approach of McCook on the Corinth road.   Hearing heavy firing in front of Rousseau, about ten o'clock, and observing it gradually gaining ground toward Shiloh Church, he moved the head of his column to General McClernand's right, formed line of battle, facing south, with Buckland next to McClernand and Stuart on his right, and advanced slowly and steadily under a heavy fire of musketry and artillery.

General Lewis Wallace discovered at dawn, on the bluff on the opposite side of Brier Creek, and just facing Thompson's battery, a hostile battery.   The Twentieth Ohio discharging their rifles to clear them, were answered by a volley that disclosed the presence of a hostile line of battle.   At the same time Pond's brigade and Ketchum's battery became aware of the fact that only the valley of Brier Creek separated them from troops that had arrived in the night.   Colonel Pond was dismayed by the further discovery that he was nearly a mile in advance of his nearest support.   After a short engagement he withdrew his infantry, leaving Wharton's regiment of mounted Texas Rangers to support the battery.   After a sharp artillery duel, Ketchum drew off his battery, covered by the mounted regiment.   General Grant directing Wallace to push his line of attack to the west, directly from the river, the division advanced, the brigades in echelon, the First to the front and left, the Third to the right and rear, sweeping the bluffs facing Snake Creek and Owl Creek, and coming out in the fields in rear of Sherman's camps.   Wheeling the division to the left, he soon became hotly engaged, first Thompson's battery with another battery, then infantry with opposing infantry.

There was yet a gap between Sherman and Wallace, but

the conflict now raged about Shiloh Church with a fury sur-
passing any portion of the battle of Sunday.   McCook, with
his well closed division, McClernand and Sherman with their
attenuated but persistent commands, Wallace with his fresh
and compact division, with the batteries of Bouton, McAllister, Wood, Thompson, and Thurber, formed a curved line
concentrating upon the convex line comprised of part of
Clark's division, Wood's brigade, Trabue's brigade, Cheatham's division, and Ruggles' division, with the batteries of
Ketchum, Byrne, Bankhead, and others.   McClernand, Sherman, and Wallace all speak with admiration of the splendid
fighting of McCook's division.   Ammunition was becoming
exhausted.   Buckland withdrew his regiments to fill their
boxes.   Stuart's brigade, now commanded by Colonel Kilby
Smith, plunged forward to make up with renewed vigor for
diminished numbers.   Wallace's left flank was exposed.
The Eleventh Indiana, changing front, faced the danger on
its flank.   The First Nebraska having used its last cartridge,
the Seventy-sixth Ohio leaped to its place.   Thompson's
battery having expended its last round, Thurber's guns took
their place so quickly that there was no intermission in the
fire.   The Twentieth Ohio, sent off to the right to meet a
force springing up in that quarter, met with a sudden discharge at close range, dashed through a fringe of bushes, and
drove a battery from the field beyond.

   Wood's brigade, charging on Rousseau, was knocked to
pieces and retired to the rear, where General Wood with the
aid of cavalry gathered up 1,500 stragglers into an ineffec-
tive reserve.   McCook pushed his line forward to Sherman's
camp.   The lines were pressed closer and the fire was hotter
than ever.   General Grant called two regiments, and in person led them in a charge in McCook's front, and broke
the enemy's line.   Endurance has its limits.   The intense

strain of two days was telling. Beauregard saw his men were beginning to flag; exhausted regiments were dropping out of line. It was now three o'clock. Two hours before, General Beauregard had sent word to his extreme right in Nelson's front, to retire slowly in alternate lines. Breckenridge, put in command of the movement, had drawn Statham's brigade from Crittenden's front. Beauregard was fighting to secure his retreat.

Colonel Thompson, aide-de-camp to Beauregard, says in his report : " While I was engaged in rallying our disorganized troops to the left and rear of the church, you seized the banners of two different regiments and led them forward to the assault in face of the fire of the enemy ; but from the feebleness of the response I became convinced that our troops were too much exhausted to make a vigorous resistance. I rode up to you and advised that you should expose yourself no further, but should dispose your troops so as to retire from Shiloh Church in good order." Colonel Whittlesey, in his report, states : " There being signs of a retreat farther to the south, Lieutenant Thurber was directed to sweep the ground in front, which he did with his two howitzers and three smooth-bores in fine style. Two prisoners captured near there, one of them an officer of the Creole Guard, state that General Beauregard was endeavoring to form a line for a final and desperate charge on our right when Lieutenant Thurber opened upon him, and the result was a disorderly retreat."

The battle was over. General Beauregard posted a battery and a brigade on the rising ground south of Oak Creek, commanding the ground about Shiloh Church, and withdrew his worn troops behind them. General Beauregard says this was at two o'clock. Cheatham fixes the hour when he retired at half-past two. The National commanders fix the close of the contest at about three o'clock. At Woods', about two miles beyond, a rear-guard took position again. At Mickey's, where Breckenridge had already arrived, he was detailed with his command as rear-guard, and the rest of the army passed on to Monterey.

There was no pursuit of the retreating army. All advance by the National troops ceased about four o'clock. McCook went into bivouac near the camp of Peabody's brigade, Prentiss' division. Wood's division, arriving too late to take part in the battle, pushed to the front and engaged his skirmishers with the light' troops covering the retreat. Mendenhall's battery, far off toward Crittenden's left, catching some glimpses of the retiring column through openings in the forest, sent some parting rounds. Wood and Crittenden went into bivouac in front of Prentiss' camp. General Buell pushed Nelson forward on the Hamburg road, near to the crossing of Lick Creek, and the division bivouacked near Stuart's camp. The divisions, or what was present of them, of McClernand, Sherman, Hurlbut, and W. H. L. Wallace, returned to their camps. Lewis Wallace advanced his division across Oak Creek to the large field. Company A, of the Twentieth Ohio, obtaining permission to proceed farther, advanced to the Confederate hospital and was deploying to drive off a detachment of cavalry that was burning a commissary train, when it was recalled to rejoin the division, then returning across Oak Creek, to bivouac in front of the camp of McDowell's brigade.

McClernand and Sherman formed part of the line of battle. Prentiss' division was gone. The other two divisions, what was left of them, acted in reserve. Hurlbut formed his division in the morning complete, with the exception of the Forty-sixth Illinois, which served for the day with McClernand. It was a skeleton division. The Third Iowa was

12

140 men under the command of a lieutenant. In the forenoon, General Grant sent Hurlbut out to act as reserve to
McClernand. The Twenty-eighth Illinois took place for a
while on McClernand's left, and Veatch with his three regiments took place on McCook's left, when he diverged from
Crittenden. Colonel Tuttle, senior officer in the Second
Division, by the death of W. H. L. Wallace and the wounding of McArthur, gathered the remaining regiments of his
division, except the Fourteenth Missouri and the Eighty-first
Ohio, added to them Colonel Crocker and three regiments
of McClernand's First Brigade, and marched in reserve to
Crittenden.   He sent the Second Iowa to Nelson, when
Nelson's line was broken by the gallant but disastrous charge
of Hazen ; the Eighth and Eighteenth Illinois moved out to
the left of Crittenden when he diverged from Nelson, and
the Seventh Iowa, moved into the front line later in the day.

The number of Johnston's army has already been given as
40,000 men. Badeau says the effective force present in the
National camps Sunday morning was 33,000 men. General
Sherman makes the number 32,000. William Preston Johnston, in the Life of his father, makes the number of the
National troops, the "grand total in Sunday's battle," 41,543.
These various statements arise from the different ways of
making and reading returns. Forty thousand does not rep-
resent the total force which A. S. Johnston led to Shiloh.
Forty thousand "present for duty" is exclusive not only of
the brigade of detailed teamsters and cooks that General
Johnston complained of, but of all regular and permanent
details.   It appears from some reports which give numbers,
that it was also exclusive of temporary details made for the
occasion of the battle—hospital men, train guards, ammunition guards, sappers and miners, infantry detailed to act
with batteries, etc. It appears from some of the reports,

which state numbers, that the "enlisted men" "present for duty," in the "Field Returns of the Confederate Forces that marched from Corinth to the Tennessee River," comprised only non-commissioned officers and privates, and was therefore exclusive of musicians, buglers, artificers, etc., though enlisted as such. The 40,000, therefore, is the number of the combatants engaged in the battle. The field return is susceptible of further explanations, the character of which does not appear. The field return, for example, gives the "present for duty," in the artillery in Polk's corps, as 20 officers and 331 enlisted men—351 in all; while the official report of the chief of artillery of the corps, of casualties in the battle, giving each battery separately, states the number actually engaged in the battle as 21 officers, 56 non-commissioned officers, and 369 privates, making a total of 446. It is clear, therefore, that the 40,000 is intended as the number of officers, non-commissioned officers, and privates actually engaged in the battle, and a comparison of the reports of General Polk's chief of artillery with the returns suggests that in some way it may not be the full number of combatants engaged.

The aggregation of returns making 41,153 present for duty in Grant's army at Pittsburg Landing, Sunday morning, is not a consolidated return, but a collection of footings of regimental returns, the nearest in date attainable to April 6th, for the most part furnished by the War Department to Colonel Johnson, the rest either taken from reports of State adjutant-generals, or else estimated. The statement includes the Fourteenth Wisconsin and the Fifteenth Michigan, neither of which arrived till after the close of Sunday's battle.* Deducting the "present for duty" given for these, 1,488, leaves, in round numbers, as in General Johnston's army,

---

* This is a mistake as to the Fifteenth Michigan, which lost, Sunday, 33 killed, 64 wounded, and 7 missing.

40,000. But "present for duty" in the returns of the National forces, includes musicians, buglers, artificers, etc; all men present for the duty for which they were enlisted. The army was clothed with music. There were 72 regiments present, including those which arrived Sunday morning. The field music of 720 companies, with the buglers of cavalry and artillery, made about three thousand men. Besides these there were bands so numerous that an order was shortly afterward made, restricting the number of bands to one to each brigade. Where the battle reports give the number taken into action, the difference in the number given and the number of "present for duty," as given by the War Department to Colonel Johnston, suggests that many had gone on to the sick list, or been detailed, between the date of the return and April 6th; or that many men present for duty were left behind in camp. Probably all were true, and thirty-three thousand or thirty-two thousand is the number of officers, non-commissioned officers, and privates actually engaged in Sunday's battle on the National side. The reinforcements of Monday numbered, of Buell's army, about twenty thousand; Lewis Wallace, sixty-five hundred; other regiments, about fourteen hundred.

There ought to be no uncertainty in the reports of casualties. Yet, while the general result is clear, precision in detail is now hardly attainable. General Beauregard's report gives his loss as 1,728 killed, 8,012 wounded, and 959 missing; making an aggregate of 10,699. Of the reported missing, many were killed or wounded. These numbers are the aggregate of losses reported by brigades. They cannot include casualties at division, corps, or army headquarters, happening either to the generals commanding, or to the officers on their staff, or to enlisted men on duty there. And while batteries were attached to brigades, the cavalry was a wholly independent command, not attached or reporting to brigades or divisions; two regiments were not attached to any corps. Their casualties cannot be included in brigade reports. Colonel Johnston, after much examination, "finds a possible variation of 218 more casualties, principally in missing, that might be added to General Beauregard's report."

The generally accepted official report of the National loss is: in Grant's army, 1,437 killed, 5,679 wounded, and 2,934 missing, making a total of 10,050; in Buell's army, 263 killed, 1,816 wounded, and 88 missing—making a total of 2,167. The two armies aggregated 1,700 killed, 7,495 wounded, and 3,022 captured—making total, 12,217. The War Department, in the printed collection of battle reports, does not give the casualties of the two armies separately, but gives the aggregate, 1,574 killed, 7,795 wounded, and 2,794 missing—making a total of 12,163. The "Medical and Surgical History of the War" makes the loss 1,735 killed, 7,882 wounded, 3,956 missing—making a total of 13,573. The loss of the Army of the Ohio, as given above, is the report of General Buell on April 15th. Six days later, the Medical Director of that army made to General Buell a tabulated statement of killed and wounded in each regiment, brigade, and division engaged, which makes the number 236 killed and 1,728 wounded. All these estimates are based upon the same material—upon the field reports. As the revisers of the reports for publication have had the best opportunity for deliberate examination and for comparison of the reports with muster-rolls, their estimate of casualties is perhaps the most trustworthy.

The loss in artillery on each side was about equal. General Sherman lost seven guns and captured seven. General McClernand lost six guns and captured three. Prentiss lost eight guns. Hurlbut lost two batteries. The Army of the Ohio captured about twenty guns, many of them being recaptured guns, lost on Sunday. One of Breckenridge's brigades threw away their arms, taking in place better arms picked up on the field. There was a great destruction of camp equipage and stores. The quartermaster of the Third Iowa, in Hurlbut's division, packed everything in wagons, safely carried stores and baggage to the landing, and let down the tents to save them from damage by shot. Before the wagons of Prentiss' division went to the rear, while the division was still engaged at the front, Colonel Miller's servant gathered everything in the Colonel's tent, packed it in one of the wagons, carried it safely off, and kept all in good order till Miller returned from captivity. But such thoughtfulness was the exception, and the returning troops found much missing and more destroyed.

Heavy rain fell again Monday night. Next morning General Grant sent General Sherman with his two brigades, and General Wood with his division and the Fourth Illinois Cavalry, in pursuit. The miry road was lined with abandoned wagons, limber-boxes, and with hospitals filled with wounded. The advance was suddenly fallen upon by Forrest and his cavalry, and driven back in confusion. Forrest coming upon the main column retired, and was pursued in turn. General Sherman advanced about a mile farther, and returned to camp. Breckenridge remained at Mickey's three days, guarding the rear, and by the end of the week Beauregard's army was again in Corinth. The battle sobered both armies. The force at Pittsburg Landing saw rudely dashed aside the expectation of speedy entry into Corinth. The force at Corinth, that marched out to drive Grant into the river, to scatter Buell's force in detail, and return in triumph to Nashville, was back in the old quarters, foiled, disheartened.

CHAPTER VIII.

CORINTH.

WHEN news of the two days' fighting was received at the North, the people of the Ohio Valley and St. Louis were stirred to active sympathy. Steamboats bearing physicians, nurses, sisters of charity, and freighted with hospital supplies were at once despatched and soon crowded the shore of Pittsburg Landing. There was need for all the aid that was brought. Besides the thousands of wounded, were other thousands of sick. The springs of surface water used in the camps, always unwholesome, were now poisonous. The wells lost their strength; of the sick many died every day. Hospital camps spread over the hills about the landing, and the little town of Savannah was turned into a hospital. Fleets descended the river bearing invalids to purer air and water.

General Halleck arrived at the landing on April 11th, established his headquarters near the river bluff, and assumed personal command. General Pope, with the Army of the Mississippi, summoned from the operations just begun before Fort Pillow, arrived on the 21st, and went into camp at Hamburg. Seasoned troops from Missouri and fresh regiments from recruiting depots arrived. The camps were pushed out farther from the river, and Halleck found 100,000 effective men under his command. The army was

organized into right wing, centre, left wing, and reserve.
The right wing comprised all the army of the Tennessee except the divisions of McClernand and Lewis Wallace, together with the division of General Thomas from the army
of the Ohio, and was commanded by General Thomas. The
remnants of the commands of Prentiss and W. H. L. Wallace were incorporated in two new divisions. The centre,
composed of the Army of the Ohio, except Thomas' division,
was commanded by General Buell. The left wing, the
Army of the Mississippi, to which General Granger's cavalry
division was still attached, was commanded by General
Pope. General Pope, General Rosecrans having been assigned to him for duty, divided his command on May 29th
into two wings, the right commanded by General Rosecrans,
the left by General Hamilton. The reserve, under General
McClernand, comprised his division and that of Lewis Wallace. General Grant was appointed second in command,
without command or duty attached to that position, though
he still remained commander of the District of West Tennessee.

Beauregard was reinforced, almost immediately after his return, by Van Dorn with 17,000 troops seasoned by campaigns
in Missouri and Arkansas, raising his effective strength to
50,000. The Confederate Government at Richmond and the
State governments in the Southwest strained every resource
to increase his force. Unimportant posts were denuded of
their garrisons, new regiments were recruited, and Price, of
Missouri, whom the Government at Richmond had refused
to recognize, was appointed major-general. Beauregard
found his force amount on the muster-rolls to an aggregate
of more than 112,000. But sickness and absence were so
prevalent that the return of effectives never quite reached
53,000. The position at Corinth was naturally strong.

Standing on a long ridge in the fork of two streams, which
run parallel to each other nearly to their junction, protected
on the front and both flanks by swampy valleys traversed by
the streams and obstructed by dense thickets, a line of earth-

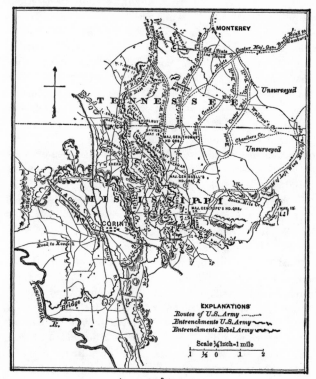

Approach to Corinth.

works running along the crest of the highland bordering
the valleys, it could be approached with difficulty. The difficulty was enhanced by a belt of timber which screened the

works from view. Railroads coming into the town facili-
tated reinforcement and supply.

Beauregard kept strong parties well advanced to his front,
while the National force at the river, absorbed in the work
of organization and supply, made little effort to ascertain
his position. As late as April 27th, a reconnoitering party
sent out by McClernand discovered that Monterey, twelve
miles from the landing, was held in some force. Next day
General Stanley, of Pope's command, sent out a detachment
that drove this force beyond Monterey. General Halleck
began his march about the close of April, moving slowly,
keeping his army compact, intrenching at every halt, and
ordering his subordinate commanders strictly to refuse to
be drawn into a general engagement. The right wing halted
and intrenched immediately beyond and to the west of Monterey on May 4th. The enemy's outposts kept close in front
of Halleck's army and opposed every advance.

General Pope, moving out on the left from Hamburg,
stretched in advance of the adjoining part of the line. On
May 3d, his command being encamped with Seven Mile
Creek in his front, General Paine, with his division, pushed
forward to Farmington, within four miles of Corinth, attacked a considerable force and drove them from their
intrenchments, compelling them to leave their dead, as well
as their tents and baggage, behind. Next day Pope advanced
his entire force within a mile and a half of Farmington, but
had to return next day to his former position behind Seven
Mile Creek, to keep up his connection with Buell. On the
8th, he again moved his whole force to Farmington, and
pushed two divisions on separate roads almost up the intrenchments at Corinth; but was again informed that the
army to his right was not ready to advance. One brigade
was still kept as advanced guard at Farmington. On the 9th,

a heavy force from Corinth emerged from the timber just as Plummer's brigade, then on post, was being relieved by Palmer's. The two brigades met the attack briskly and a severe combat ensued. Pope's army was within a mile and a half behind the creek, but forbidden by Halleck's order to cross. To prevent a general engagement, the two brigades were withdrawn. It was not till after May 20th that Pope finally occupied Farmington with Buell's line.

Observing indications on the night of the 26th, he next day advanced, and connecting with his right, sent Colonel W. L. Elliot, of the Second Iowa Cavalry, with his own regiment, commanded by Lieutenant-Colonel E. Hatch, and the Second Michigan Cavalry, commanded by Colonel P. H. Sheridan, who was only assigned to the regiment that day, to make a circuit around Corinth and strike the railroad forty miles in its rear, doing all practicable destruction to it. Next day, the 28th, Stanley's division was pushed far forward and after a sharp skirmish secured possession of a ridge directly upon the creek, in front of the enemy's works, which he at once fortified. Paine's division was moved out the same day and occupied on Stanley's left. The same day Buell advanced Nelson and Crittenden to the front on a line with Stanley.

General Thomas held Sherman on his extreme right, with his skirmishers extended out to sweep the Mobile & Ohio Railway.

After several successive advances, meeting more or less opposition, on May 17th, Sherman moved with his division —supported by Hurlbut—and with batteries, against a commanding position in his front, called Russell's, just two miles from the main entrenchments, held by a brigade. It was some time before he could get a position for his batteries. Resistance was more obstinate than at any previous en-

counter. But, finally, the point was carried, and was found
to cover a sweep of open ground to the south, the direction
toward Corinth, and the division entrenched. Beyond the
open land—stretching southward from Russell's—and intervening woods was other open land, and still beyond, a rising
ground, with a high wooded ridge behind it. On this rising
ground was a loop-holed, double loghouse, having complete
command of the open ground north of it. A force stationed
here exceedingly annoyed Sherman's pickets. On the morning of the 27th he moved with his division and batteries,
supported by Veatch's brigade, from Hurlbut, and John A.
Logan's brigade, from McClernand, quietly and unseen
through the timber as near as practicable. Two of Silversparre's twenty-pounder Parrott guns were moved silently
through the forest to a point behind a hill, from the top of
which could be seen the house and ground to be contested.
The guns were unlimbered, loaded, and moved by hand to
the crest. A quick rapid fire demolished the house. The
infantry dashed forward, drove the enemy from the ridge
across a field and into a thick forest beyond. In the afternoon the repulsed troops suddenly reappeared, but after a
short contest they were again driven. The advanced position thus carried was at once intrenched. The intervening
forest concealed from Sherman the fact that, though he was
more than three miles from the town, he was now less than
a mile from the main defences of Corinth, that he was between the creeks, and there was no obstruction but the forest
between him and the works. Next day General Thomas advanced the rest of his command, wheeling it to the right so
as to bring the whole upon the bank of the creek, which
flowed between him and Corinth. This advance brought his
left division, T. W. Sherman, within half a mile of the main
entrenchments, but separated from them by the swampy

valley. The same day Buell advanced McCook to connect with T. W. Sherman. Halleck had been a month gaining with his 100,000 men a few miles, but he was now closing in upon Corinth.

Beauregard, though contesting pertinaciously every advance, had already began his evacuation. Detailed instructions, regulating the evacuation and the subsequent march of the troops, were issued on the 26th and 27th, and three o'clock A.M. of the 29th was appointed for the time. On the 28th an order was issued postponing the movement till the morning of the 30th, to gain more time for removing stores. On the 29th the final order was issued, which required, among other precautions to hide the movement, "whenever the railroad-engine whistles during the night, near the intrenchments, the troops in the vicinity will cheer repeatedly, as though reinforcements had been received." The sick and wounded were sent off by railway, as was the heavy artillery. All valuable stores were carried off; though considerable quantities of stores of all kinds—commissary, quartermaster, and ordnance—were neither removed nor destroyed. Elliot, with his cavalry, struck the railroad at Booneville before daylight of the 30th, destroyed there a locomotive, twenty-five box-cars loaded with ordnance, ammunition, and quartermaster stores, one or two platform-cars with field-pieces, a depot building filled with ordnance stores, tore up the track and destroyed two culverts, and returned to Farmington, having prevented the further use of that railway for the purposes of evacuation.

General Pope, hearing the engines whistling and men cheering after midnight, understood it as Beauregard intended—to show the arrival of reinforcements. But skirmishers were sent forward to ascertain, if practicable, the fact. Trains were heard leaving, and, at six o'clock, explosions, followed by clouds of smoke, satisfied both him and Sherman that Beauregard was leaving. By eight o'clock, his advance had felt their way through the intrenchments and marched into town. Sherman, having farther to go, was but little later in entering.

Pope's army moved at once in pursuit along the roads leading south — Rosecrans in front, Hamilton following, and Granger with the cavalry keeping in advance. Two divisions from Thomas' command, Davies and T. W. Sherman, were added to the pursuing column. The pursuit developed the fact that Beauregard, or a large part of his force, halted at Baldwin, fifty miles south of Corinth, in an inaccessible position behind swamp and jungle, while his line extended to the northwest, to Blackland, an approachable point west of the railroad. Pope had made all preparations to attack at Blackland and issued the order, when Buell arrived at the front and suspended the attack. Beauregard retreated farther and the pursuing force returned to Corinth.

General Pope, while detained a few days at Danville, by illness, was continually receiving despatches from his officers at the front, and telegraphing them or their substance to General Halleck, at Corinth, a few miles off. General Granger said in one despatch there were ten thousand stragglers from the retreating army in the woods, all of whom would come in and surrender. All knew the woods were full of stragglers, and it was generally believed that General Granger's estimate of their number and intentions was reasonable. Pope, condensing into one, despatches received from Rosecrans, Hamilton, and Granger, telegraphed to Halleck, "The two divisions in the advance under Rosecrans are slowly and cautiously advancing on Baldwin this morning, with the cavalry on both flanks. Hamilton, with two divisions, is at Rienzi, and between there and Booneville, ready to move forward, should they be needed. One brigade from the reserve occupies Danville. Rosecrans reports this morning that the enemy has retreated from Baldwin, but he is advancing cautiously. The woods, for miles, are full of stragglers from the enemy, who are coming in in squads. Not less than ten thousand men are thus scattered about, who will come in within a day or two." General Halleck despatched to the War Department "General Pope, with 40,000 men, is thirty miles south of Corinth, pushing the enemy hard. He already reports 10,000 prisoners and deserters from the enemy, and 15,000 stand of arms captured." This despatch of General Halleck's made a great sensation. The expectation that the stragglers would come into the National camp was disappointed; the prisoners taken were few, and Pope was censured for making a statement of fact which he neither made nor authorized.

Fort Pillow was abandoned June 1st. On June 6th, Admiral Davis, who had succeeded Commodore Foote, destroyed the Confederate fleet in front of Memphis after an engagement of an hour and a half. The same day, the two regiments that Pope left with the fleet, entered the city. The objects proposed in the spring were accomplished, though not in the manner designed. The railway connection at Corinth was broken, though not by a mere dash from the river. Fort Pillow was possessed, Memphis was occupied, and the Mississippi open to Vicksburg. The volunteers had been through a hard military school. After their experience in fighting, they had practice in the slow advance to Corinth, in picket duty and field fortification. They had learned something of the business of war and were now ready for campaign, battle, and siege.

END.

INDEX.